DAVE BARRY

is

not

making

this

up

DAVE BARRY

is

not

making

this

up

BY DAVE BARRY

CARTOONS BY JEFF MacNELLY

FAWCETT COLUMBINE · NEW YORK

A Fawcett Columbine Book
Published by Ballantine Books

http://www.randomhouse.com

This edition published by arrangement with Crown Publishers, Inc.

The essays in this collection were originally published in *The Miami Herald*.

Library of Congress Catalog Card Number: 94-90797

ISBN: 0-449-90973-5

Cover design by Kristine Mills
Cover photo by Bill Wax

Manufactured in the United States of America

First Ballantine Books Edition: May 1995

20 19 18 17 16 15 14 13 12 11

To Earnest, who was a big help;
and to Zippy, who was a small
emergency backup help

CONTENTS

INTRODUCTION

People often say to me: "Dave, you are a leading journalism professional and not as short as I expected. What is your secret of success?"

The answer is that, throughout my career, I have always kept one vital journalistic principle foremost in my mind: *Try not to leave the house.* A journalist who leaves his or her house can run into all kinds of obstacles, including:

- Editors.
- Members of the public.
- News events involving actual facts.

All of these obstacles can seriously interfere with the basic work of journalism, which is sitting around and thinking stuff up. This is what I mainly do, which is why I have been able to achieve a level of high-quality journalistic productivity, as measured in booger jokes, that a guy like David Broder can only dream about.

Nevertheless, every now and then a situation will come up wherein a story of major importance is breaking somewhere other than in my office, and I have no choice but to go and cover it. For example, in this book you will find a column concerning an incident in 1992 when I left my house and traveled, without regard for my personal convenience or safety, all the way to my yard, to see the World's Fastest Lawn Mower. That's the kind of dedicated professional I am.

The result is that this book contains a number of columns based on real events. There are also some longer articles, most of which originally appeared in the *Miami Herald*'s Sunday magazine, *Tropic;* these also contain an unusually high (for me) level of factual content. That's why this book is called *Dave Barry Is* Not *Making This Up.**

I want to stress, however, that this title does not mean that this is a serious book. This book also contains a lot of "tongue-in-cheek" social commentary and satire, by which I mean lies. I hope you don't find this mixture of fact and fiction to be confusing. If, in reading the following pages, you are uncertain as to whether a specific statement is meant seriously or not, simply apply this rule of thumb: If the statement makes you consider filing a lawsuit, I was kidding. Ha ha!

---

* In an effort to boost sales, we were going to call it *Rush Limbaugh Is* Not *Making This Up*, but there was some kind of legal problem.

■ READER ALERT ■

The following section, which is mostly about family stuff, contains the article that pretty much launched my writing career: the story of my son's "natural" birth. When I wrote it back in 1981, Beth and I were living in Glen Mills, Pennsylvania, and I had a job teaching effective business-writing seminars.* I wrote the article for the *Philadelphia Inquirer*, and it got reprinted in many other newspapers, including the *Miami Herald*, which ended up hiring me. So in a way you could say that I owe my job to my son. Although if you consider the amount of money I wound up spending just on He-Man action figures, I have more than paid him back.

---

* This could be why we got so far behind Japan.

FOOD FOR THOUGHT

It's getting late on a school night, but I'm not letting my son go to bed yet, because there's serious work to be done.

"Robert!" I'm saying, in a firm voice. "Come to the kitchen right now and blow-dry the ant!"

We have a large ant, about the size of a mature raccoon, standing on our kitchen counter. In fact, it *looks* kind of like a raccoon, or possibly even a mutant lobster. We made the ant out of papier-mâché, a substance you create by mixing flour and water and newspapers together into a slimy goop that drips down and gets licked up by your dogs, who operate on the wise survival principle that you should immediately eat everything that falls onto the kitchen floor, because if it turns out not to be food, you can always throw it up later.

The ant, needless to say, is part of a Science Fair project. We need a big ant to illustrate an important scientific concept, the same concept that is illustrated by *all* Science Fair projects, namely: "Look! I did a Science Fair project!"

(I know how we can solve our national crisis in educational funding: Whenever the schools needed money, they

could send a letter to all the parents saying: "Give us a contribution right now, or we're going to hold a Science Fair." They'd raise billions.)

Our Science Fair project is due tomorrow, but the ant is still wet, so we're using a hair dryer on it. Science Fair judges *hate* a wet ant. Another problem is that our ant is starting to sag, both in the front (or, in entomological terms, the "prognosis") and in the rear (or "butt"). It doesn't look like one of those alert, businesslike, "can-do" ants that you see striding briskly around. It looks depressed, like an ant that has just been informed that all 86,932 members of its immediate family were crushed while attempting to lift a Tootsie Roll.

While Robert is drying the ant, I get a flashlight and go outside to examine the experiment portion of our project, which is entitled "Ants and Junk Food." On our back fence we put up a banner that says, in eight-inch-high letters, WELCOME ANTS. Under this is a piece of cardboard with the following snack substances scientifically arranged on it: potato chips, a spicy beef stick, a doughnut, a Snickers candy bar, chocolate-filled cookies, Cheez Doodles, Cocoa Krispies, and Screaming Yellow Zonkers. If you were to eat this entire experiment, you would turn into a giant pimple and explode.

We figured this experiment would attract ants from as far away as Indonesia, and we'd note which junk foods they preferred, and this would prove our basic scientific point ("Look! I did a Science Fair project!"). Of course you veteran parents know what actually happened: The ants didn't show up. Nature has a strict rule against cooperating with Science Fair projects. This is why, when you go to a Science Fair, you see 200 projects designed to show you how an electrical circuit works, and not one of them can actually make the little bulb light up. If you had a project that was supposed to demonstrate the law of gravity using heavy lead weights, they would fall *up*. So when the ants saw our banner, they said: "Ah-hah! A Science Fair project! Time for us to act in a totally unnatural manner and stay away from the food!"

The irony is, I knew where some ants were: in my office. They live in one of the electrical outlets. I see them going in there all day long. I think maybe they're eating electrons, which makes me nervous. I seriously considered capturing one of the office ants and carrying it out to the science experiment, and if necessary giving it broad hints about what to do ("Yum! Snickers!"). But I was concerned that if I did this, the ants might become dependent on

4

me, and every time they got hungry they'd crawl onto my desk and threaten to give me electrical stings if I didn't carry them to a snack.

Fortunately, some real outdoor ants finally discovered our experiment, and we were able to observe their behavior at close range. I had been led to believe, by countless public-television nature shows, that ants are very organized, with the colony divided into specialized jobs such as drones, workers, fighters, bakers, consultants, etc., all working together with high-efficiency precision. But the ants that showed up at our experiment were total morons. You'd watch one, and it would sprint up to a Cocoa Krispie, then stop suddenly, as if saying: "Yikes! Compared with me, this Cocoa Krispie is the size of a Buick!" Then it would sprint off in a random direction. Sometimes it would sprint back; sometimes it would sprint to another Cocoa Krispie and act surprised again. But it never seemed to *do* anything. There were thousands of ants behaving this way, and every single time two of them met, they'd both stop and exchange "high-fives" with their antennas, along with, I assume, some kind of ant pleasantries ("Hi Bob!" "No, I'm Bill!" "Sorry! You look just like Bob!"). This was repeated *millions of times*. I watched these ants for two days, and they accomplished *nothing*. It was exactly like highway construction. It wouldn't have surprised me if some ants started waving orange flags to direct other insects around the area.

But at least there were ants, which meant we could do our project and get our results. I'd tell you what they were, but I really think you should do your own work. That's the whole point of a Science Fair, as I keep telling my son, who has gone to bed, leaving me to finish blow-drying the ant.

FATHER FACES LIFE

A Long-Overdue Attack on Natural Childbirth

Let's take just a quick look at the history of baby-having. For thousands of years, only women had babies. Primitive women would go off into primitive huts and groan and wail and sweat while other women hovered around. The primitive men stayed outside doing manly things, such as lifting heavy objects and spitting.

When the baby was born, the women would clean it up as best they could and show it to the men, who would spit appreciatively and head off to the forest to throw sharp sticks at small animals. If you had suggested to primitive men that they should actually watch women have babies, they would have laughed at you and probably tortured you for three or four days. They were real men.

At the beginning of the 20th century, women started having babies in hospital rooms. Often males were present, but they were professional doctors who were paid large sums of money and wore masks. Normal civilian males continued to stay out of the baby-having area; they remained in waiting rooms reading old copies of *Field and*

Stream, an activity that is less manly than lifting heavy objects but still reasonably manly.

What I'm getting at is that, for most of history, baby-having was mainly in the hands (so to speak) of women. Many fine people were born under this system. Charles Lindbergh, for example.

Things changed, though, in the 1970s. The birth rate dropped sharply. Women started going to college and driving bulldozers and carrying briefcases and freely using such words as "debenture." They just didn't have time to have babies. For a while there, the only people having babies were unwed teenage girls, who are very fertile and can get pregnant merely by standing downwind from teenage boys.

Then, young professional couples began to realize their lives were missing something: a sense of stability, of companionship, of responsibility for another life. So they got Labrador retrievers. A little later, they started having babies again, mainly because of the tax advantages. These days you can't open your car door without hitting a pregnant woman. But there's a catch: *Women now expect men to watch them have babies.* This is called "natural childbirth," which is one of those terms that sounds terrific but that nobody really understands. Another one is "pH balanced."

At first, natural childbirth was popular only with hippie-type, granola-oriented couples who lived in geodesic domes and named their babies things like Peace Love World Understanding Harrington-Schwartz. The males, their brains badly corroded by drugs and organic food, wrote smarmy articles about what a Meaningful Experience it is to see a New Life Come Into the World. None of these articles mentioned the various other fluids and solids that come into the world with the New Life, so people got

7

the impression that watching somebody have a baby was just a peck of meaningful fun. At cocktail parties, you'd run into natural-childbirth converts who would drone on for hours, giving you a contraction-by-contraction account of what went on in the delivery room. They were worse than Moonies or people who tell you how much they bought their houses for in 1973 and how much they're worth today.

Before long, natural childbirth was everywhere, like salad bars; and now, perfectly innocent civilian males all over the country are required by federal law to watch females have babies. I recently had to watch my wife have a baby.

First, we had to go to 10 evening childbirth classes at the hospital. Before the classes, the hospital told us, mysteriously, to bring two pillows. This was the first humiliation, because no two of our pillowcases match and many have beer or cranberry-juice stains. It may be possible to walk down the streets of Kuala Lumpur with stained, unmatched pillowcases and still feel dignified, but this is not possible in American hospitals.

Anyway, we showed up for the first class, along with about 15 other couples consisting of women who were going to have babies and men who were going to have to watch them. They all had matching pillowcases. In fact, some couples had obviously purchased tasteful pillowcases especially for childbirth class; these were the trendy couples, wearing golf and tennis apparel, who were planning to have wealthy babies. They sat together through all the classes, and eventually agreed to get together for brunch.

The classes consisted of sitting in a brightly lit room and openly discussing, among other things, the uterus. Now I can remember a time, in high school, when I would have *killed* for reliable information on the uterus. But having discussed it at length, having seen actual full-color *diagrams,* I must say in all honesty that although I respect it a great deal as an organ, it has lost much of its charm.

Our instructor was very big on the uterus because that's where babies generally spend their time before birth. She also spent some time on the ovum, which is near the ovaries. What happens is the ovum hangs around reading novels and eating chocolates until along comes this big crowd of spermatozoa, which are very tiny, very stupid one-celled organisms. They're looking for the ovum, but most of them wouldn't know it if they fell over it. They swim around for days, trying to mate with the pancreas and whatever other organs they bump into. But eventually one stumbles into the ovum, and the happy couple parades down the Fallopian tubes to the uterus.

In the uterus, the Miracle of Life begins, unless you believe the Miracle of Life does not begin there, and if you think I'm going to get into that, you're crazy. Anyway, the ovum start growing rapidly and dividing into lots of little specialized parts, not unlike the federal government. Within six weeks, it has developed all the organs it needs to drool; by 10 weeks, it has the ability to cry in restaurants. In childbirth class, they showed us actual pictures of a fetus developing inside a uterus. They didn't tell us how these pictures were taken, but I suspect it involved a great deal of drinking.

We saw lots of pictures. One evening, we saw a movie of a woman we didn't even know having a baby. I am serious. Some woman actually let moviemakers film the whole thing. In color. She was from California. Another time, the instructor announced, in the tone of voice you might use to tell people they had just won free trips to Hawaii, that we were going to see color slides of a cesarean section. The first slides showed a pregnant woman cheerfully entering the hospital. The last slides showed her cheerfully holding a baby. The middle slides showed how they got the baby out of the cheerful woman, but I can't give you a lot of detail here because I had to go out for 15 or 20 drinks of water. I do remember that at one point our instructor cheerfully observed that there was "surprisingly little blood, really." She evidently felt this was a real selling point.

When we weren't looking at pictures or discussing the uterus, we practiced breathing. This is where the pillows came in. What happens is that when the baby gets ready to leave the uterus, the woman goes through a series of what the medical community laughingly refers to as "contractions." If it referred to them as "horrible pains that make you wonder why the hell you ever decided to get pregnant," people might stop having babies and the medical community would have to go into the major-appliance business.

In the old days, under President Eisenhower, doctors avoided the contraction problem by giving lots of drugs to women who were having babies. They'd knock them out during the delivery, and the women would wake up when their kids were entering the fourth grade. But the idea with natural childbirth is to try to avoid giving the woman a lot of drugs, so she can share the first, intimate moments after birth with the baby and the father and the obstetrician and the pediatrician and the standby anesthesiologist and several nurses and the person who cleans the delivery room.

The key to avoiding drugs, according to the natural-childbirth people, is for the woman to breathe deeply. Really. The theory is that if she breathes deeply, she'll get all relaxed and won't notice that she's in a hospital delivery room wearing a truly perverted garment and having a baby. I'm not sure who came up with this theory. Whoever it was evidently believed that women have very small brains. So, in childbirth classes, we spent a lot of time sprawled on these little mats with our pillows while the women pretended to have contractions and the men squatted around with stopwatches and pretended to time them. The trendy couples didn't care for this part. They were not into squatting. After a couple of classes, they started bringing little backgammon sets and playing backgammon when they were supposed to be practicing breathing. I imagine they had a rough time in actual childbirth, unless they got the servants to have contractions for them.

Anyway, my wife and I traipsed along for months, breathing and timing, respectively. We had no problems whatsoever. We were a terrific team. We had a swell time. Really.

The actual delivery was slightly more difficult. I don't want to name names, but I held up *my* end. I had my stopwatch in good working order and I told my wife to breathe. "Don't forget to breathe," I'd say, or, "You should breathe, you know." She, on the other hand, was unusually cranky. For example, she didn't want me to use my stopwatch. Can you imagine? All that practice, all that squatting on the natural-childbirth classroom floor, and she suddenly gets into this big snit about stopwatches. Also, she almost completely lost her sense of humor. At one point, I made an especially amusing remark, and she tried to hit me. She usually has an excellent sense of humor.

Nonetheless, the baby came out all right, or at least all right for newborn babies, which is actually pretty awful unless you're a fan of slime. I thought I had held up well when the doctor, who up to then had behaved like a perfectly rational person, said, "Would you like to see the placenta?" Now let's face it: That is like asking, "Would you like me to pour hot tar into your nostrils?" *Nobody* would *like* to see a placenta. If anything, it would be a form of punishment:

JURY: We find the defendant guilty of stealing from the old and the crippled.

JUDGE: I sentence the defendant to look at three placentas.

But without waiting for an answer, the doctor held up the placenta, not unlike the way you might hold up a bowling trophy. I bet he wouldn't have tried that with people who have matching pillowcases.

The placenta aside, everything worked out fine. We ended up with an extremely healthy, organic, natural baby, who immediately demanded to be put back into the uterus.

All in all, I'd say it's not a bad way to reproduce, although I understand that some members of the flatworm family simply divide into two.

PUMPED UP

You want to know what's wrong with America? I'll tell you what's wrong: too many kinds of sneakers.

This problem was driven home to me dramatically when my 10-year-old son decided to join a track club. At first I was in favor of this, because I was a track man myself back at Pleasantville High School, where in 1965—and I hope I do not sound too boastful here—I set a New York State record for Shortest Time on a Track Team Before Quitting.

My original goal was to obtain a varsity letter. I needed one because at the time I was madly in love with Ann Weinberg, who would have been the ideal woman except for one serious flaw: She was an excellent athlete. On an average afternoon she would win the state championship in about nine sports. When we had the annual school awards assembly, various teams would troop on and off the auditorium stage, but Ann would just remain up there, getting honored, until all you could see was a large, Ann-shaped mound of trophies.

This caused painful feelings of inadequacy in me, a

small, chestless, insecure male whose only recognized high-school athletic achievement was the time when, through an amazing physical effort, I managed to avoid ralphing directly onto the shoes of the principal as he was throwing me out of a pep-rally dance for attempting to sleep under the refreshments table. Unfortunately this is not the kind of achievement for which you get a varsity letter.

So in a desperation effort to impress Ann, I joined the track team. This meant I had to go into the locker room with large, hairy jocks who appeared way too old for high school. I bet you knew guys like that. At the time I thought that they had simply matured faster than I had, but I now

realize that they were actually 40-year-old guys who chose to remain in high school for an extra couple of decades because they enjoyed snapping towels at guys like me. They are probably still there.

I was under the impression that all you had to do, to obtain your varsity letter, was spend a certain amount of time in the locker room, but it turned out that they had a picky rule under which you also had to run or jump or hurl certain objects in an athletic manner, which in my case was out of the question, so I quit.

However, during my brief time on the team I did learn some important lessons that have stayed with me throughout life, the main one being that if you are on the track-team bus, and the coach comes striding down the aisle and demands to know which team member hurled the "moon"—which is NOT one of the approved objects that you hurl in track—out the bus window at the police officer who is now threatening to arrest the entire team, you should deny that you saw anything, because it's better to go to jail than to betray the sacred trust of your teammates and consequently be forced to eat a discus.

So I was glad that my son became interested in this character-building sport, until he announced that he needed new sneakers. This troubled me, because he already HAD new sneakers, which cost approximately as much as an assault helicopter but are more technologically advanced. They are the heavily advertised sneakers that have little air pumps inside. This feature provides an important orthopedic benefit: It allows the manufacturer to jack the price way up. Also it turns the act of walking around into a highly complex process. "Wait!" my son will say, as we're rushing off to school, late as usual. "I have to pump more air into my sneakers!" Because God forbid you should go to school underinflated.

So I figured that high-powered sneakers like these would be fine for track, but both my wife and my son gently informed me that I am a total idiot. It turns out you don't *run* in pump sneakers. What you do, in pump sneakers, is pump your sneakers. For running, you need *a completely different kind* of sneakers, for which you have to pay a completely different set of U.S. dollars.

Not only that, but the sneaker salesperson informed me that, depending on the kind of running my son was going to do, he might need *several kinds* of sneakers. The salesperson's tone of voice carried the clear implication that he was going to call the Child Abuse Hotline if I didn't care enough, as a parent, to take out a second mortgage so I could purchase sufficient sneakerage for my son.

I have done a detailed scientific survey of several other parents, and my current estimate is that sneakers now absorb 83 percent of the average U.S. family income. This has to stop. We need Congress to pass a law requiring the sneaker industry to return to the system we had when I was growing up, under which there was only one kind of sneakers, namely U.S. Keds, which were made from Army surplus tents and which cost about $10, or roughly $1 per pound. This simple act would make our nation strong again. Slow, but strong. Probably your reaction is, "Dave, that's an excellent idea, and you should receive, at minimum, the Nobel Prize." Thank you, but as an American, I am not in this because I seek fame and glory. All I seek, as an American, is a varsity letter.

DIRTY DANCING

My son, who is 11, has started going to dance parties. Only minutes ago he was this little boy whose idea of looking really sharp was to have all the Kool-Aid stains on his He-Man T-shirt be the same flavor; now, suddenly, he's spending more time per day on his hair than it took to paint the Sistine Chapel.

And he's going to parties where the boys dance with actual girls. This was unheard of when I was 11, during the Eisenhower administration. Oh, sure, our parents sent us to ballroom-dancing class, but it would have been equally cost-effective for them to simply set fire to their money.

The ballroom in my case was actually the Harold C. Crittenden Junior High School cafeteria. We boys would huddle defensively in one corner, punching each other for moral support and eyeing the girls suspiciously, as though we expected them at any moment to be overcome by passion and assault us. In fact this was unlikely. We were not a fatally attractive collection of stud muffins. We had outgrown our sport coats, and we each had at least one shirttail elegantly sticking out, and the skinny ends of our

17

neckties hung down longer than the fat ends because our dads had tied them in the only way that a person can tie a necktie on a short, fidgety person, which is by standing behind that person and attempting several abortive knots and then saying the hell with it. Many of us had smeared our hair with the hair-smear of choice in those days, Brylcreem, a chemical substance with the natural look and feel of industrial pump lubricant.

When the dance class started, the enemy genders were lined up on opposite sides of the cafeteria, and the instructor, an unfortunate middle-aged man who I hope was being paid hundreds of thousands of dollars, would attempt to teach us the Fox Trot.

"ONE two THREE four ONE two THREE four," he'd say, demonstrating the steps. "Boys start with your LEFT foot forward, girls start with your RIGHT foot back, and begin now ONE . . ."

The girls, moving in one graceful line, would all take a step back with their right foot. At the same time, on the boys' side, Joseph DiGiacinto, who is now an attorney, would bring his left foot down firmly on the right toe of Tommy Longworth.

"TWO," the instructor would say, and the girls would all bring their left foot back, while Tommy would punch Joe sideways into Dennis Johnson.

"THREE," the instructor would say, and the girls would shift their weight to the left, while on the other side the chain reaction of retaliation had spread to all 40 boys, who were punching and stomping on each other, so that our line looked like a giant centipede having a Brylcreem-induced seizure.

This was also how we learned the Waltz, the Cha Cha, and—this was the instructor's "hep cat" dance step—the Lindy Hop. After we boys had thoroughly failed to master these dances, the instructor would bring the two lines together and order the boys to dance directly with the girls, which we did by sticking our arms straight out to maintain maximum separation, lunging around the cafeteria like miniature sport-coat-wearing versions of Frankenstein's monster.

We never danced with girls outside of that class. At social events, girls danced the Slop with other girls; boys made hilarious intestinal noises with their armpits. It was the natural order of things.

But times have changed. I found this out the night of Robby's first dance party, when, 15 minutes before it was time to leave for the party, he strode impatiently up to me, wearing new duds, looking perfect in the hair department, and smelling vaguely of—Can it be? Yes, it's *Right Guard!*—and told me that we had to go *immediately* or we'd be late. This from a person who has never, ever shown the slightest interest in being on time for anything, a person who was three weeks late to his own *birth.*

We arrived at the dance-party home at the same time as Robby's friend T.J., who strode up to us, eyes eager, hair slicked.

"T.J.!" I remarked. "You're wearing *cologne!*" About two gallons, I estimated. He was emitting fragrance rays visible to the naked eye.

We followed the boys into the house, where kids were dancing. Actually, I first thought they were jumping up and down, but I have since learned that they were doing a dance called the Jump. We tried to watch Robby, but he gestured violently at us to leave, which I can understand. If God had wanted your parents to watch you do the Jump, He wouldn't have made them so old.

Two hours later, when we came back to pick him up, the kids were slow-dancing. Of course the parents weren't allowed to watch this, either, but by peering through a window from another room, we could catch glimpses of couples swaying together, occasionally illuminated by spontaneous fireballs of raw hormonal energy shooting around the room. My son was in there somewhere. But not my little boy.

A LEFT-HANDED
COMPLIMENT

I was feeling good that morning. I woke up to the happy discovery that not a single one of our major home appliances had broken during the night and we still had running water, which is highly unusual in our household. Then I got both dogs all the way outside without getting the Weewee of Joy on my feet. It looked like it was going to be a great day.

Then, like a fool, I picked up the newspaper. You should never pick up a newspaper when you're feeling good, because every newspaper has a special department, called the Bummer Desk, which is responsible for digging up depressing front-page stories with headlines like DOORBELL USE LINKED TO LEUKEMIA and OZONE LAYER COMPLETELY GONE DIRECTLY OVER YOUR HOUSE.

On this particular morning the story that punched me right in the eyeballs was headlined: LEFTIES' LIVES SHORTER? STUDY SAYS SO. You probably read about this. Researchers did a study showing that left-handed people live an average of *nine years less* than right-handed people. This was very alarming to me because I'm left-handed, along with 10 percent of the population, as well as many famous historical figures such as Napoleon, Leonardo da Vinci, Sandy Koufax, Speedy Alka-Seltzer, and Flipper. President Bush is also left-handed, which has raised a troublesome constitutional issue because every time he signs a bill into law he drags his hand through his signature and messes it up. Nobody knows whether this is legal. "This doesn't look like a signature," observed the Supreme Court, in one recent case. "This looks like somebody killed a spider on the Federal Highway Authorization Act."

Because of the way we write, most of us lefties go through life with big ink smears on the edges of our left

hands. In fact, when I first saw the newspaper article about lefties dying sooner, I thought maybe the cause would be ink absorption. Or maybe it would be related to the fact that we spent our entire academic careers sitting with our bodies twisted clockwise so we could write on those stupid right-hand-only desks. I have this daydream wherein the inventor of those desks is shipwrecked on a remote island, and some natives come out of the jungle, and he waves at them in what he thinks is a friendly manner, unaware that this is the fierce Wagoondi tribe, and if you wave at them with your *left* hand, they treat you like a god, but if you wave with your *right* hand, they play the Happy Snake Game with your intestines. Not that I am bitter. Nor am I bitter about the fact that I always got bad grades in art class because I couldn't work scissors designed for right-handed people. On Parents' Night, when all the children's art projects were put up for display, mine was the one that looked as though the paper had been chewed to pieces by shrews.

Nor am I bitter about gravy ladles. And if you don't understand WHY I'm not bitter about gravy ladles, just try using one with your left hand.

But I have to admit that I AM a little bitter about this business of dying nine years early. According to the researchers, a major reason for this is that left-handers have a lot more accidents than right-handers. I know why this is: We read books backward. Really. When left-handers pick up books, they tend to start reading from the last page. This saves us a lot of time with murder mysteries, but it's a bad habit when we're reading, say, the instructions for operating a barbecue grill, and we begin with "STEP 147: IGNITE GAS."

I myself have always been accident-prone, especially when I attempt to use tools designed for right-handed people, the extreme example being chain saws, which should not even be legal to sell to left-handers. I had one back during the Energy Crisis, when I had installed a wood-burning stove in our fireplace in an effort to reduce our energy consumption by covering the entire household with a thick, insulating layer of soot. Near our house was a large tree, which I realized could supply our soot needs for the better part of the winter. So one day I strode out and, drawing on my skills as an English major, started making strategic cuts designed to cause the tree to fall away from the house. I even called my wife out to watch the tree fall, and of course those of you who are familiar with situation comedies have already figured out what happened: The tree, which was clearly right-handed, fell in the *exact wrong direction,* chuckling audibly all the way down and missing the living room by maybe six inches.

My wife, who thought I had *planned* to have the tree do this, said, "That was great!" And I replied, "Wurg," or words to that effect, because my brain was busy trying to get my heart going again. Speaking of which: Some scientists think that left-handed people's brains work completely differently from right-handed people's brains. I read an article once that theorized that left-handers are a different species from right-handers. Isn't that silly? As if we were *aliens* or something. What nonsense! Planet foolish this over take will we day one.

READER ALERT

What follows is a story I wrote in 1988 about a spate of UFO sightings in the town of Gulf Breeze, Florida. The sightings eventually gained national attention, and there are still a lot of people in the UFOlogy community who believe that Gulf Breeze is frequented by extraterrestrials. The guy I identified only as "Ed" in this story is Ed Walters; he became a big name on the UFO circuit and wrote a book. A number of people have claimed that Walters perpetrated a hoax; in 1990, a man living in Walters's former house said he found a model of a UFO—which looked like the one in Walters's photos—in the attic.

A SPACE ODYSSEY

OK, there is definitely something strange going on in Gulf Breeze, Florida. The two most likely explanations are:

1. Somebody is perpetrating a hoax and a bunch of other people, through inexperience, imagination, or ignorance, are falling for it.
2. Intelligent beings from elsewhere in the universe, driving craft with fantastic capabilities, have come to Earth, and they are observing us, and they have a Paralysis Ray and—this is going to make some South Floridians nervous—they apparently speak Spanish.

    After spending a few days in Gulf Breeze checking things out, I've decided for myself which of these two possible explanations is closest to the truth. Here's the story as far as I know it; see what you think.

THE WIRE STORY

On December 3, the *Herald* published this item in a roundup of wire-service stories from around the state:

GULF BREEZE—Pictures of what was labeled as a glowing unidentified flying object published in the November 18 edition of the *Sentinel* of Gulf Breeze have prompted a half-dozen residents to report similar sightings.

Duane B. Cook, editor and publisher of the weekly, said the object looks like the top of the Space Needle in Seattle, but he hopes it's an alien spacecraft. He said the state's Mutual UFO Network will examine the three photos taken November 11 near the town that appeared with a letter written by the anonymous photographer.

Here at Tropic we are always on the lookout for stories of potentially intergalactic significance, so I immediately checked the *Herald* files to see if any other strange unexplained phenomena had been reported in the Gulf Breeze area. You can imagine how my pulse quickened when I discovered that:

- On December 5, at The Zoo, a privately operated zoo in Gulf Breeze, a wedding ceremony was held for giraffes. This really happened. Their names are Gus and Gigi.
- On August 19, a Gulf Breeze man was bitten by a pygmy rattlesnake as he (the man) examined a potted plant in the garden shop of the Wal-Mart store in nearby Fort Walton Beach. Just two days later, at a Wal-Mart in North Fort Myers, a woman examining a potted hibiscus was bitten by another pygmy rattlesnake. Wal-Mart officials were unable to explain this rash of pygmy-rattler attacks and described it as "unusual."

Well, of course, I needed no further convincing. I grabbed my camera—you have to be ready—hopped on a plane and was off to conduct my investigation.

THE TOWN OF GULF BREEZE

Gulf Breeze is a small residential community just across a bridge from Pensacola, way at the far western end of Florida, almost in Alabama. It is the opposite of Miami, geographically and in many other ways. It is not even in the same time zone as Miami. Miami is in the Eastern Time Zone and Gulf Breeze is in about 1958. In Gulf Breeze, when you buy something at a store, the counterperson usually smiles and says, "Y'all come back 'n' see us now, n'kay?" Whereas in Miami, the counterperson doesn't usually say anything because he or she is having a very important personal telephone conversation that cannot be interrupted just for some idiot customer.

I begin my investigation by driving through downtown Gulf Breeze. Even at slow speed, this takes less than five minutes. It appears to be a normal beach-oriented town, very quiet in the off-season. There are a lot of things in the sky, because this is an area of extremely heavy air traffic: Nearby, besides the commercial airport in Pensacola, are the Pensacola Naval Air Station, Eglin Air Force Base, and several other airfields. Almost any time you look up, you see a plane or a helicopter. In looking around, however, the only phenomenon I notice that does not seem to have an obvious earthly explanation is a bumper sticker that says BUSH 88.

But you never can tell. As you know if you ever watched "The Twilight Zone," there are times when everything seems to be perfectly normal, and then suddenly, without warning, something happens, something that you know is somehow . . . wrong, and you start to hear that piercing high-pitched electronic-sounding "Twilight Zone" music—*deedeedeedee deedeedeedee*—and the hairs on the back of your neck, even if you use extra-hold styling mousse, stand on end.

Little do I realize, as I drive through the quiet town of Gulf Breeze, that before I leave, I am going to experience that very feeling. More than once.

THE NEWSPAPER

My first stop is the *Gulf Breeze Sentinel*. The *Sentinel* is a weekly newspaper with a circulation of 3,500, soaring to 4,500 in the summer. It is not the kind of paper that practices the kind of snide, cynical, city-slicker style of journalism exemplified by this article. It's the kind of newspaper where many stories consist mostly of local people's names. You can get into the *Sentinel* merely by having your birthday. Also there are many photographs of local boards, clubs, civic groups, etc., engaging in planning activities. In the November 19 issue, there's a front-page photograph of a man smiling and holding up, for no apparent reason, bags of Hershey's Kisses, accompanied by the caption:

> Dave Bozeman, manager of the Piggly Wiggly, is planning now for the Annual Gulf Breeze Christmas Parade. Piggly Wiggly plans to have several entrics, including the Folgers Race Cars and, of course, the Pig!

In short, the *Sentinel* seems to be your basic small hometown paper doing hometown stories about hometown people. Except that in the same November 19 issue, right above the Piggly-Wiggly manager, is a story headlined:

UFO SIGHTED OVER GULF BREEZE

Below this are three photographs of this thing, shaped roughly like a fat disk with a glowing, tapered bottom and a small, glowing protrusion on top. There are regularly spaced dark marks going around the side. The thing is in fairly clear focus. It appears to be hovering in the evening sky; you can see the dark blurred shapes of trees in the foreground.

The "story" accompanying the photographs consists entirely of the text of an anonymous letter to the newspaper, allegedly written by the photographer, who says he took five Polaroid pictures of the thing from his yard on the night of November 11.

"I was reluctant at first to show [the photographs] to any one," says the letter, ". . . but my wife convinced me to show them to Ed. Ed in turn said that the photos should be shown to the press. . . . I am a prominent citizen of the community, however, and need anonymity at this time. I know what I saw and would feel much better if I knew I was not alone.

"Let me reassure you that this is not a hoax."

It was "Ed" who brought the photographs to the *Sentinel,* according to Duane Cook, the editor and publisher. Cook, 43, is a former computer salesman who took over the paper from his stepfather in 1980. Cook thought the pictures looked convincing, and "Ed," whom Cook knows, said the photographer was responsible. So Cook decided to go ahead with the story, but he was still "nervous a little" about it until the morning of November 19, when the paper was just about to go to press. On that day Cook's stepfather and predecessor as editor, Charles Somerby, and his wife (Cook's mother), Doris Somerby, stopped by the paper. Cook showed them the Polaroids.

They did not act surprised.

They said they had seen the same object.

On the same night.

Deedeedeedee deedeedeedee

"I lost all fear of going to press with it," Cook says.

THE WITNESSES

If you called up Central Casting and asked for two people to play the parts of the Reliable Witnesses, they would send you Charlie and Doris Somerby. He's 69 and, before his newspaper career, served as a naval communications officer in World War II and Korea. She's 67 and holds the world indoor record for grandmotherliness (when I visit their home to interview them, she has an actual apple pie cooling on the kitchen table).

The Somerbys say that on November 11, while taking a walk at sundown, they saw an object out over the bay headed toward Gulf Breeze. It made no sound, they say, and it did not look like any kind of aircraft they had ever seen. They watched for some mention of it on the evening TV news, but there was none. Until Cook showed them the photographs, they had not planned to say anything about it.

I ask them, several times and in several ways, if they're sure that the thing they saw over the bay looks the same as the object in the photographs. They say they're sure. Driving away, I am convinced they're telling the truth.

THE STORY SPREADS

When the *Sentinel* published the UFO pictures, people started calling. "We got a half a dozen calls from people who saw something that night," says Cook. His staff started collecting these reports, and ran them as a front-page story in the November 25 issue. A local TV station did a story about the UFO, showing one of the Polaroids blown way up. "That was impressive," says Cook.

Then another local TV station did a story about it.

Then United Press International did a story about it.

And then it happened, the event that distinguishes an

interesting but basically local story from a story with potentially shocking Worldwide Implications: The *National Enquirer* called.

Yes. The paper that is frequently way ahead of the media pack on major Hollywood divorces; the paper that obtained and published the now-historic photograph showing Donna Rice sitting on Gary Hart's lap because he was too much of a gentleman to push her off; the paper that once offered a reward of $1 million for "positive proof" that extraterrestrial spacecraft are visiting the Earth; this paper was now calling Duane Cook of the *Gulf Breeze Sentinel*.

The *Enquirer* sent a reporter, who wanted to take the photographs back to the paper's home base in Lantana, Florida, for further analysis. But by that point Cook had been in touch with the state director of the Mutual UFO Network (more on this later), who had advised Cook that these photographs could be very valuable and he should not let them out of his sight. So the *Enquirer* flew Cook down to Lantana, where, Cook says, "They gave [the photographs] the most thorough going-over, and they couldn't find any flaws." They made Cook an offer: $5,000 for the right to publish the photographs before anybody else—if the *Enquirer* decided to use them. But before they made that decision, they wanted a second opinion. So they flew Cook and his photographs all the way to the world-famous NASA Jet Propulsion Laboratory at Cal Tech in Pasadena, California. There, Cook says, "they took a series of photographs of the photographs," the idea being that they would analyze them further and give the results to the *Enquirer*.

Five thousand dollars. NASA. This was getting very exciting. And there was more to come.

Two more photographs arrived at the *Sentinel*. These were taken with a 35mm camera, and although the quality is worse than that of the Polaroids, they appear to show the same object. An anonymous letter claims the photographs were taken in June of 1986—over a year before the Polaroids were allegedly taken.

Then somebody stuffed a manila envelope into the *Sentinel* mailbox containing nine more photographs; again the quality is poor, but they appear to show the same object. The accompanying letter is signed "Believer Bill," who claims he took the pictures with a toy camera—which also was stuffed into the envelope—that his children had left in his car.

Then "Ed"—remember "Ed"? The one who brought in the original photographs?—gave the *Sentinel* a very clear Polaroid that he says he took in his backyard; it shows, very clearly, three of the objects.

At this point the *Sentinel* was turning into the Galactic Clearing House for UFO Evidence. The photographs had become so common that the last two sets, which seemed to suggest that a regular alien invasion was going on right there in Gulf Breeze, ran on page four of the December 24 issue. The page-one story was the Christmas parade.

But Duane Cook, the editor, is hoping that the UFO story isn't over.

"I would be delighted if, whoever they are, they have decided to communicate, because they've been watching us for some time now," he tells me. "My main fear is that we won't be adult enough to welcome them. My contribution would be to condition people's minds to the possibility that they do exist, so that we can learn from them.

In fact, maybe . . ."—Cook pauses, then shakes his head—
". . . no, that sounds grandiose."

"What?" I ask.

"Well," he says, looking at me carefully, "maybe that's
why I'm here."

Deedeedeedee deedeedeedee

THE UFO PEOPLE

Duane Cook is not alone. A lot of people are convinced
that extraterrestrials are watching us. There are more than
200 UFO-oriented organizations worldwide, according to
The UFO Encyclopedia, which bills itself as "a comprehen-
sive A-to-Z guide to the UFO phenomenon" and which
cheerfully and uncritically passes along all kinds of fascinating UFO stories. Here, for example, is an excerpt from
the entry about a "contactee"—a person who claims to
receive regular visits from extraterrestrials—named Howard Menger:

> According to Menger, a rash of sightings around his
> New Jersey home was followed by regular social visits
> from the Space People. He performed favors for his
> alien friends and even acted as their barber, cutting
> their long blond hair in order that they could pass
> unnoticed among the earthlings. Menger was re-
> warded with a trip to the moon, where he breathed
> easily in a surface atmosphere similar to Earth's. He
> brought back some lunar potatoes, which reportedly
> contained five times the protein found in terrestrial
> potatoes. Their nutritive value could not be proved,
> however, because Menger had supposedly handed
> them over to the U.S. government, which was keep-
> ing them a secret.

Not all the UFO believers, however, are Froot Loops. A
lot of people who definitely qualify as Responsible Citi-

zens have claimed they saw something strange in the sky. In 1973, Jimmy Carter, then the governor of Georgia, reported that he had seen a UFO in 1969, just before a Lions Club meeting (although we should bear in mind that, as president, Carter claimed he was attacked by a large swimming rabbit). Other celebrities who, according to *The UFO Encyclopedia,* have reported UFO sightings include: Jackie Gleason, Muhammad Ali, John Travolta, Elvis Presley, Orson Bean, and, of course, William Shatner.

Many "sightings" have turned out to be hoaxes. Many others have turned out to be man-made or natural objects—airplanes, weather balloons, satellites, planets, stars, etc. And some remain unexplained. The mainstream scientific community tends to believe these are probably ordinary phenomena that could, with sufficient information, be identified. The UFOlogists tend to believe they are evidence that extraterrestrials are here. The debate rages on.

The federal government has, reluctantly, played a major role in the UFO controversy. The Air Force, in an operation called Project Blue Book, collected and investigated UFO reports from 1948 until 1969, when the project was dropped because, the government says, it was a waste of time. Many UFOlogists, however, argue that the government wasn't really trying to solve the mystery but to discredit the witnesses, and is now engaged in a massive conspiracy to cover up evidence of extraterrestrial visits, just as it has refused to release the lunar potatoes. Some of the conspiracy theories are pretty spooky, as we will see.

THE MAN FROM MUFON

On my second day in Gulf Breeze, I drive out to Fort Walton Beach, about 40 miles east, to visit Donald Ware, the Florida state director for the Mutual UFO Network

(MUFON). MUFON describes itself as "an international scientific organization composed of people seriously interested in studying and researching" in an effort to provide "the ultimate answer to the UFO enigma."

Ware, who spent 26 years in the Air Force and flew two combat tours as a fighter pilot, appears to be a very straight arrow, a serious man with serious eyes. And he takes the Gulf Breeze sightings very seriously. After a MUFON field investigator—there are more than 50 in the state—examined the Polaroids and interviewed some of the witnesses, MUFON released a "preliminary evaluation" stating that the Polaroids show "an unknown of great significance."

Ware tells me that this is going to be "an important case that will be discussed by UFOlogists all over the world." As he talks, he backs up various points by pulling papers from his files, which he began amassing back in 1952, when he saw lights over Washington, D.C., in what turned out to be a famous UFO incident.

"After 12 years of study," he says, "I decided that somebody was watching us. After 10 more years of study, I concluded that someone in our government has known this since 1947."

Solemnly, Ware hands me a book containing a reproduction of what are alleged to be Top Secret U.S. government documents. These documents state that in 1947, near Roswell, New Mexico, the U.S. government secretly recovered a crashed flying saucer and four alien bodies.

And President Harry Truman set up a secret group of top scientists, called "Majestic 12," to study the aliens and their craft.

And this whole thing has been kept secret ever since.

Ware is looking at me intently.

"Well!" I say brightly. "Thanks very much for your help!"

THE KEY FIGURE

I'm sitting in my motel room, thinking. The more I think, the more it seems to me that, whatever is going on in Gulf Breeze, the Key Figure is "Ed." He's the one who brought the first set of Polaroids to the *Sentinel,* allegedly on behalf of the photographer. He's the one, according to Duane Cook, who took the later Polaroid showing three objects. He's the only photographer who isn't totally anonymous. I decide I need to talk to him. I call Cook, the *Sentinel* editor, and ask him to ask "Ed" to please get in touch with me.

Less than an hour later, I hear a tapping at my motel window.

THE VISIT

"Ed" does not introduce himself, except to say: "I'm the guy you're looking for." He's about my age, 40. He's articulate, mechanically inclined, and very sharp.

We talk for about an hour. Right away he admits he took the first set of Polaroids. He says he invented the story about being the intermediary because he was afraid that if his name got in the paper, he'd be ridiculed. "I have a family," he says. "I'm a successful businessman. Everyone in this town knows me."

"I know what I saw is real," he says.

He becomes more agitated as he talks. He tells me he has seen the UFO six times. He says that what has been published in the *Sentinel* is only the beginning of the story.

"There is more," he says. "But it's scary."

He leans forward.

"There is this thing," he says, "and it can shoot a blue beam out of it. I got a picture of it doing it."

He shows me the picture. It's another Polaroid, show-

37

ing the now-familiar object, with what appears to be a faint bluish ray of light coming out of the hole in the bottom.

Now the conversation gets weird. "Ed" says he was once trapped in the beam. Frozen. Paralyzed. Couldn't move a muscle.

While he was in the beam, "Ed" believes, the UFO beings put some kind of "mental input" into his brain, so they could communicate with him, but something—jets, maybe—scared them off, and now the beings keep coming around because they're trying to get the mental input back. He knows when they're nearby. "I can hear a hum," he says.

He also hears voices, speaking in Spanish and some kind of strange "consonant language." He has heard the voices at night, near his house, out by his pool pump. He wishes that, whoever they are, they would hurry up and take their mental input back and leave him alone.

"This has f—— up the last two months of my life," he says.

I tell him that a lot of people would say he was crazy, or lying.

He says he knows that, but he has something that will shut everybody up.

He says he has a videotape.

Deedeedeedee deedeedeedee

THE VIDEOTAPE

Later that day, shortly past dusk, a *Herald* photographer and I go to see "Ed." He lives in a comfortable suburban house in a tidy development. His wife is in the kitchen, cooking dinner. She doesn't come out to greet us. I get the impression she's not thrilled that we're there.

"Ed," on the other hand, is very cordial. He laughs a lot. He bustles around, showing us a drawing he made of the UFO and getting out more photographs of it. He seems to have a lot more of them. He shows us the camera he uses, an old, battered Polaroid held together with tape.

Then the three of us sit on his living room floor, and he shows us the videotape, which he shot with his Sony home video camera. The tape was apparently taken in his backyard, from behind some bushes, which can be heard rustling as the photographer moves around. The tape shows the same object, just above the tree line, moving kind of jerkily from right to left, then back again. It lasts only a minute or two.

"Ed" shows it to us again, then looks at us.

"That's incredible," we say, almost simultaneously.

THE QUESTIONS

As soon as we leave, the photographer tells me that something is wrong. The film "Ed" uses in his Polaroid has an ASA rating of 80, which means it is relatively slow to react to light. This means that the shutter must stay open a relatively long time, especially in low light. And this in turn means that a moving object, even if photographed by a skilled photographer, would look blurred. "Ed" has stated repeatedly that the object moves almost constantly—as it does in the videotape—and yet in almost all of his photographs, the object is in fairly sharp focus.

"It just doesn't look right," says the photographer.

Neither does the videotape, at least to my eyes. The jerky motion of the object makes it appear small, almost toylike, and fairly close, although "Ed" insists it is "as big as a house."

Some other things are strange. Why, if "Ed" could sense the impending arrival of the object, didn't he ever call his neighbors to be witnesses? And why, when he realized the object was visiting repeatedly, didn't he get a better camera? I asked him both of these questions several times; he never really answered.

But the most troubling evidence is "Ed" himself. He acts agitated, manic. Not to put too fine a point on it, he acts a little crazy. Of course, maybe this is normal behavior if aliens have put a mental input in your head. But still, I am getting skeptical. And I am not alone.

THE SKEPTIC

Philip Klass is the nation's, if not the world's, leading UFO skeptic. The UFOlogists do not like him (MUFON's Donald Ware suggested to me that Klass has a "mental problem"). Klass retired last year after 35 years as senior electronics editor of *Aviation Week* magazine, but his involvement with UFOs is through an organization called the Committee for the Scientific Investigation of Claims of the Paranormal, of which he is chairman of the UFO subcommittee. In that capacity, he has spent a lot of time debunking various UFO claims. For example, he recently issued a report charging that the "Majestic 12" documents—the ones that allegedly prove that the government has dead aliens stashed away—are obvious forgeries. I must admit I found that story a tad hard to believe myself. It's not that I don't believe the government would try to hide dead aliens; it's that I don't think the government would succeed, since every time the government tries to do anything secretly, as in the Iran-contra arms deal, it winds up displaying all the finesse and stealth of an exploding cigar at a state funeral. If there really were dead aliens, I figure, there also would be daily leaks about it from High-Level Officials, and huge arguments among influential congresspersons over whose district the multimillion-dollar Federal Dead Alien Storage Facility would be located in.

Anyway, Klass, as you might imagine, is very dubious about the claim that UFOs are extraterrestrial visitors.

"I can think of no more exciting story," he says, "than to say I have investigated a UFO case for which there was no earthly explanation. In the 22 years I have been investigating, I have never found a single such case."

But what about the photographs?

"Photographs are the easiest things in the world to fake," says Klass. "Even the UFO believers are very, very skeptical of them." Klass is especially suspicious of Polaroids, because they have no negatives, which are often useful in the detection of hoaxes. He thinks it's suspicious that no negatives were included with any of the photographs anonymously submitted to the *Sentinel*.

"The odds against those photographs being authentic are jillions to one," he says.

But what about the witnesses?

"Once the report gets out that there are UFOs in the area, you get all kinds of me-tooers," Klass says. "Ninety-eight percent of all people who report seeing UFOs are trying to be honest. But we've been brainwashed by what we've read and been told. And eyewitness testimony is notoriously unreliable."

That's also the opinion expressed by astronomer Robert Young in a letter to the newsletter of the Astronomical League. Young says that, having investigated "a couple of hundred UFO reports"—all of which turned out to have prosaic explanations—he has concluded that "no eyewitness report of a UFO can be taken at its face value." He adds that "waves" of UFO sightings "end when editors tire of them. . . . My experience is that when news stories stop, the calls stop too."

THE JET PROPULSION LABORATORY

I call Dr. Robert Nathan at the Jet Propulsion Laboratory. He's the one the *Enquirer* flew the Polaroids, Duane Cook and all, out to see. He's the one who's supposed to be doing the scientific photographic analysis. Only he's not. He says he's suspicious of the photographs, both because of the way they look and because more than one set of them came from the same source.

"I'm way off in the nonbeliever corner on this one," says Dr. Nathan. "Unless something changes, I don't care to use government equipment on this. I have the feeling that somebody is perpetrating a hoax."

THE RAY PEOPLE

If it is a hoax, the question is, Why? I am no psychiatrist, but I think the answer is suggested by John Keel, author of several UFO books. Keel argues that the modern era of UFO sightings was launched by a pulp science-fiction magazine called *Amazing Stories,* edited by a man named Raymond Palmer. In 1947, Palmer published a story about fiendish alien beings controlling life on Earth through the use of rays. Suddenly, *Amazing Stories* was deluged with mail from readers who insisted that the story was true, because they had been affected by the beings.

"Palmer had accidentally tapped a huge, previously unrecognized audience," writes Keel. "Nearly every community has at least one person who complains constantly to the local police that someone—usually a neighbor—is aiming a terrible ray gun at their house or apartment. This ray, they claim, is ruining their health, causing their plants to die, turning their bread moldy, making their hair and teeth fall out and broadcasting voices into their heads. Psychiatrists are very familiar with these 'ray' victims and relate the problem with paranoid schizophrenia.

"In earlier times, [the paranoiacs] thought they were hearing the voice of God and/or the devil. Today they often blame the CIA or space beings for their woes. . . . Ray Palmer unintentionally gave thousands of these people focus for their lives."

THE CALL

Back in Miami, I call "Ed" one morning. I tell him my theory, which is that he really does think he's being hounded by aliens but that he has faked all the photographs, using different cameras, in an effort to get others to believe him.

"Ed" tells me that since I last saw him, he was attacked by the beam while he was driving alone. "I was blown off the road and had to crawl underneath the truck," he says. He says he gave a full report on this to the people at MUFON, for their ever-growing data bank.

He also says that two armed men from the "Special Security Services" of the Air Force (he didn't get their names) came around with a "material seizure warrant" and demanded his photographs. He says he didn't want to send them to Duane Cook, so he told them he gave the photographs to me.

So that's the situation in Gulf Breeze, as far as I know it. Of course, there are some unanswered questions. For example, if "Ed" is faking the photographs, how is he doing it? And—this one still bothers me—what did the Somerbys see?

As of this writing, I haven't seen anything about this in the *National Enquirer*. I also haven't heard from the Air Force.

I expect, however, that I'll hear from you out there in Readerland. One thing nobody disputes is that stories about UFOs generate reports about UFOs. But listen: If you have anything to report, the place to send it is:

> The Miami UFO Center
> P.O. Box 313
> Opa-locka, FL 33054

The important thing is: Don't call me. OK? It's not that I don't believe you. It's that my life is already filled with bizarre, inexplicable phenomena, such as the way the right rear speaker in my car never works except when they play songs I hate.

Deedeedeedee deedeedeedee

READER ALERT

This next section is mostly columns about Amazing but True things that I found out about thanks to mail from alert readers. One of these readers, as you will see, is a member of the U.S. Supreme Court, who alerted me about a groundbreaking new antiflatulence product called Beano. This resulted in a column that some newspapers found too offensive to print, a fact that resulted in *another* column, which was either about censorship or circumcision, I am still not sure which.

This section also contains vital information about an issue that everybody needs to think about more, namely, toilet snakes.

PLUMBER'S HELPER

Here at the Bureau of Animal Alarm we have received a disturbing Associated Press photograph sent in by alert journalist Russ Williams of the Asheville, North Carolina, *Citizen-Times* (motto: "A Newspaper Whose Staff Has Too Much Spare Time"). This photo shows a goat, looking fairly calm under the circumstances, hanging by its horns from a rope going through a pulley attached to the side of a building. Two men in a window are holding the other end of the rope. Here is the caption, which we are not making up:

> SPAIN—A goat hangs by his horns from the bell tower of the church in Manganeses de la Polvorosa, some 200 miles northwest of Madrid. Villagers, who open the religious festival of St. Vincent by dropping a goat from the church belfry, attacked police who tried to block the tradition. The goat was uninjured as villagers caught the goat with a tarp.

As sensitive and broad-minded humans, we must never allow ourselves to be in any way judgmental of the reli-

gious practices of other people, even when these people clearly are raving space loons. We are sure that the people of Manganeses de la Polvorosa would be amused by some common American religious practices.

"We may drop goats from belfries," they'd probably say, "but at least we don't thank the Lord for touch-downs."

Nevertheless, we here at the Bureau feel that the Immigration authorities should keep a sharp lookout for Manganeses de la Polvorosa tour groups coming to the United States, particularly New York. Because they might decide to visit the Empire State Building, and while they're up on the observation deck they might suddenly smack their foreheads and realize that it's time to open the festival of St. Vincent, and the next day's *New York Post* might print the following tragic headline:

B-A-A-A-D GOAT!

TERRIFIED CROWD FLEES

120 MPH DEATH BUTT

Another animal menace that we all need to be more concerned about is giant toilet snakes. This is a growing problem, as can be seen by the following statistics:

Number of Articles About Giant Toilet Snakes We Received Prior to 1992: Zero.

Number of Articles About Giant Toilet Snakes We Have Received in 1992: One.

Statistically, this represents an increase of infinity percent in the number of giant toilet-snake reports. The most recent one, sent by alert reader Jack Sowers, was written by reporter Mike Leggett for the *Austin* (Texas) *American-Statesman*. It concerns a man named Steve Ashenfelter, who used to manage an Oklahoma hunting and fishing club. One day he went into the clubhouse bathroom, and, in his words, "there was a big snake lying in the toilet. As soon as he saw me he just swirled around and went down the pipes."

So Ashenfelter did exactly what you would do; namely, he moved to another continent.

No, really, he followed standard toilet-snake procedure, which is to go around flushing the three clubhouse toilets in an effort to get the snake to come out.

"I went in the bathroom upstairs, and there he was, lying in the toilet up there," Ashenfelter recalled. "So I went and flushed all the toilets, and he came back up in the toilet where I saw him the first time."

Eventually, Ashenfelter got the snake, but it took him two days, and he ended up using—we are still not making this up—two fishing poles, chlorine bleach, muskrat traps in all three toilets, an eight-foot piece of lumber, rope, and heavy metal hooks. The snake turned out to be over seven feet long.

We do not wish to create a nationwide panic, but apparently there is a new breed of large, commode-dwelling snakes that have *figured out how to move from toilet to toilet,* which means they could easily travel across the country via the Interstate Plumbing System. This has serious ramifications, especially if you're a parent trying to potty-train a small child. Psychologists agree that the best way to handle this situation is: lie. "Don't worry!" you should tell the small child many times. "A big snake won't come out of the toilet!" This is the approach Mister Rogers is taking.

Meanwhile, however, something must be done. One practical approach would be for the government to require all U.S. citizens to put muskrat traps in their commodes. The only problem here is that if the trap is not removed prior to commode usage, there could be severe consequences for guys of the male gender. On the other hand, many women might view this as a fair punishment for all the billions of times that guys have left the seat up. It's definitely something to think about as each of us, in his or her own way, prepares to celebrate the festival of St. Vincent.

WATCH YOUR REAR

As you are aware if you follow international events, over the past year I have written a number (two) of columns about the worldwide epidemic of snakes in toilets. As a result I have received many letters from people who have had personal toilet-snake encounters, to the point where I now consider it newsworthy when somebody reports NOT finding a snake in a toilet.

But now I am getting nervous. I say this because of a recent alarming incident wherein a woman, attempting to use her commode, was attacked in an intimate place—specifically, Gwinnett County, Georgia—by a *squirrel*. I have here an article from the *Atlanta Journal-Constitution*, written by Gail Hagans and sent in by a number of alert readers. The headline—a textbook example of clear journalism—states: *Squirrel somehow makes way into commode, scratches Gwinnett woman's behind*. I am not making this headline up.

The woman is quoted as follows: "I went to the bathroom and lifted the lid and sat down. That's when I felt something scratching my behind."

So, following the recommended "Jump, Slam, Call, and Tell" emergency procedure, she jumped up, slammed the lid down, called her husband at work, and told him to come home immediately, which he of course did. We may live in an age of gender equality, but men have a protective instinct that dates back millions of years, to when they would have had to defend their mates from such vicious predators as the saber-toothed tiger and the mastodon (toilets were much bigger in those days).

Unfortunately, by the time the husband got home, the squirrel had drowned, forcing us to once again ask WHEN the failed Clinton administration will demand that ALL commodes be equipped with tiny life preservers. But that

is not the issue at hand. The issue at hand is that the squirrel apparently got into the plumbing system via a roof vent, which means that if you, like so many people, have a roof, your toilet is vulnerable to ANY organism with a long, narrow body, including (but not limited to) otters, weasels, dachshunds, squids, and international fashion models with only one name, such as Iman.

But that is by no means the only major toilet development. There is also the Mystery Toilet in Texas that produces ballpoint pens. I am not making this up, either. According to a story in the *Wichita Falls* (Texas) *Times/Record News,* written by Steve Clements and sent in by several alert readers, a man named David Garza of Henrietta, Texas, has fished 75 Paper Mate ballpoint pens out of his toilet over the past two years, sometimes as many as five pens per day. Garza has no idea where they're coming from, and neither do the local sewer authorities.

The story was accompanied by a photograph of Garza sitting on the bathtub next to the Mystery Toilet, holding a pen, looking like a successful angler. I called him immediately.

"What's the status of the toilet?" I asked.

"It's still a mystery," he said. He said he hadn't found any new pens since the newspaper story, but that he has become something of a celebrity. This is understandable. People naturally gravitate to a man who has a Mystery Toilet.

"Everywhere I go," he said, "people say to me, 'Hey, you got a pen?' "

I asked him if the pens still write, and he said they do.

"Paper Mate ought to make a commercial out of this," he said. "The slogan could be, 'We come from all over and write anywhere.' You know, like Coca-Cola, 'It's there when you need it.' "

Actually, I don't think that's Coca-Cola's slogan. But Garza's statement got me to thinking about a possible breakthrough TV commercial wherein an athlete is standing in the locker room, sweating, thirsty as heck, and the toilet gurgles, and up pops a nice refreshing can of Coke. Yum! A commercial like that might be exactly what Coca-Cola needs to counteract all the free media attention Pepsi got recently with the syringe thing.

But the question is: Why are Paper Mate pens showing up in this toilet? There's only one logical explanation— I'm sure you thought of it—*alien beings*. David Garza's toilet is apparently connected to some kind of intergalactic sewage warp, through which aliens are trying to establish communication by sending Paper Mate pens (which are for sale everywhere). Probably they want us to write down our phone number on a piece of Charmin and flush it back to them.

Speaking of toilets and communication, you need to know about a TV-review column from the *Daily Yomiuru*, an English-language newspaper published in Japan. The column, sent in by alert reader Chris Graillat, states that there's a children's TV show in Japan called "Ugo Ugo Ruga," which features—I am still not making this up— "an animated character with heavy eyebrows called Dr. Puri Puri (Dr. Stinky), a piece of talking excrement that keeps popping up from the toilet bowl to express strange platitudes only an adult can fathom."

You're thinking: "Hey! Sounds like Henry Kissinger!"

No, seriously, you're thinking that there are indeed some scary worldwide developments occurring in toilets, and the international authorities had better do something about it. And then they'd better wash their hands.

IT'S A GAS

Recently, I received a letter from a justice of the United States Supreme Court concerning a product called Beano.

I absolutely swear I am not making this up. The letter, written on official U.S. Supreme Court stationery, comes from Justice John Paul Stevens, who states:

"Having long been concerned about the problem of exploding cows, it seemed imperative to pass on to you the enclosed advertisement, the importance of which I am sure will be immediately apparent to you."

Justice Stevens enclosed an advertisement from *Cooking Light* magazine for Beano, which, according to the manufacturer, "prevents the gas from beans." The advertisement includes pro-Beano quotations from various recognized intestinal-gas authorities, including (I am still not making this up) the *New York Times*, the *Idaho Statesman*, and Regis Philbin. The advertisement calls Beano "a scientific and social breakthrough," and states: "It's time to spill the Beano."

I was already aware of this product. I don't wish to toot my own horn, so to speak, but thanks to the efforts of

hundreds of alert readers, my office happens to be the World Clearinghouse for information relating to gas buildups that cause explosions in animals, plants, plumbing, humans, etc. In recent months I've received newspaper reports of explosions involving a flounder, a marshmallow, a mattress, two wine bottles, several pacemakers (during cremation), countless toilets, a flaming cocktail called a "harbor light," chicken livers, snail eggs, a turkey, a tube of Poppin' Fresh biscuits, a raccoon, and a set of breast implants.

So needless to say, many readers had already alerted me about Beano. Several of them had sent me actual samples of Beano, which comes in a small plastic bottle, from which you squirt drops onto your food. But until I got Justice Stevens's letter, I had not realized that this was a matter of concern in the highest levels of government. When you see the Supreme Court justices, they always appear to be extremely solemn, if not actually deceased. It never occurs to you that, under those robes, *they have digestive systems, too.* But they do, as can be seen by a careful reading of the transcript of a recent court hearing:

CHIEF JUSTICE REHNQUIST: Is the court to understand, then, that the counsel's interpretation of the statute is . . . All right! Who sliced the Limburger? *(He glares at the other justices.)*

JUSTICE SCALIA: Well, I am not naming names, but I happened to be glancing at the liberal wing of the court, and I definitely saw some robes billow, if you catch my drift.

JUSTICE BLACKMUN: Oh, sure, and I suppose the conservative wing doesn't sound like the All-Star Kazoo Band over there. My opinions are blowing off the bench.

JUSTICE O'CONNOR: Oh, yeah? Well, why don't you take your opinions and . . .

This is bad for America. We need our highest judicial body to stop this childish bickering and get back to debating the kinds of weighty constitutional issues that have absorbed the court in recent years, such as whether a city can legally force an exotic dancer to cover her entire nipple, or just the part that pokes out.

So I decided, as a tax-deductible public service, to do a Beano Field Test. To make sure the test was legally valid, I asked a friend of mine, Paul Levine, who's a trained attorney as well as an author, if he'd participate. Paul is a selfless, concerned citizen, so I was not surprised at his answer.

"Only if you mention that my critically acclaimed novel

To Speak for the Dead is now available in paperback," he said.

"I'm afraid I can't do that," I said. But Paul agreed to participate in the Field Test anyway, because that is the kind of American he is. My wife, Beth, also agreed to participate, although I want to stress that, being a woman, she has never, ever, in her entire life, not once, produced any kind of gaseous digestive byproduct, and when she does she blames it on the dogs.

To make this the most demanding field test possible, we went to a Mexican restaurant. Mexican restaurants slip high-octane beans into virtually everything they serve, including breath mints. It is not by mere chance that most of Mexico is located outdoors.

Paul, Beth, and I applied the Beano to our food as directed—three to eight drops per serving—and we ate it. For the rest of the evening we wandered around to various night spots, awaiting developments. Other people at these night spots were probably having exciting, romantic conversations, but ours went like this:

ME: So! How's everyone doing?

BETH: All quiet!

PAUL: Not a snap, crackle, or pop!

Anyway, the bottom (Har!) line is that Beano seems to work pretty well. Paul reported the next day that all had been fairly calm, although at 3:30 A.M. he was awakened by an outburst. "You're familiar with the Uzi?" was how he put it. I myself was far safer than usual to light a match around, and Beth reported that the dogs had been unusually quiet.

So this could be an important product. Maybe, when you go to a restaurant, if you order certain foods, the waiter should bring Beano to your table, instead of those stupid utility-pole-sized pepper grinders. "Care for some

Beano?'' the waiter could say. "Trust me, you'll need it."

And getting back to Justice Stevens's original concern, I think federal helicopters should spray massive quantities of Beano on the nation's dairy farms, to reduce the cow methane output. And of course it should be *mandatory* in the dining rooms of the United States Congress. I'm sure the Supreme Court will back me up on this.

THE UNKINDEST
CUT OF ALL

I want to warn you right away that today's topic involves an extremely mature subject matter that might offend your community standards, if your community has any.

I became sensitive about community standards recently when, at the suggestion of no less than a U.S. Supreme Court justice, I wrote a column about a ground-breaking antiflatulence product called Beano. Some newspapers—and I do not wish to name names, but two of them were the *Portland Oregonian* and the *St. Louis Post-Dispatch*—refused to print this column on the grounds that it was tasteless and offensive. Which of course it was, although it was *nothing* like the disgusting trash you hear from the Senate Judiciary Committee.

Anyway, those readers who have community standards should leave the room at this time, because today's topic is: circumcision. This is a common medical procedure that involves—and here, in the interest of tastefulness, I am going to use code names—taking hold of a guy's Oregonian and snipping his Post-Dispatch right off. This is usually done to tiny guy babies who don't have a clue as to what is about to happen. One minute a baby is lying happily in his little bed, looking at the world and thinking what babies think (basically, "Huh?"), and suddenly along comes a large person and *snip* WAAAAHHH the baby is dramatically introduced to the concept that powerful strangers can fill his life with pain for no apparent reason. This is excellent training for dealing with the Internal Revenue Service, but it's no fun at the time.

Most of us guys deal with this unpleasant experience by eventually erasing it from our conscious minds, the way we do with algebra. But some guys never get over it. I base this statement on a *San Jose Mercury News* article, written by

Michael Oricchio and mailed to me by many alert readers, concerning a group of men in California who are very upset about having been circumcised as babies. They have formed a support group called RECAP. In the interest of good taste I will not tell you what the *P* in RECAP stands for, but the "RECA" part stands for "Recover A."

According to the article, the members (sorry!) of RECAP are devoted to restoring themselves to precircumcision condition "through stretching existing skin or by surgery." I swear I am not making this up. Here is a quotation from RECAP co-founder R. Wayne Griffiths:

"There are a lot of men who are enraged that they were violated without their consent and they want to do something about it. I've always been fascinated by intact men. I just thought it looked nicer. I had friends growing up who were intact. I thought, 'Gee, that's what I'd like to be.'"

The article states that, to become intact again, Griffiths invented a 7½-ounce skin-stretching device that "looks like a tiny steel barbell," which he taped to the end of his Oregonian and wore for "four to 12 hours every day, except weekends, for a year." Using this method, he grew himself an entirely new Post-Dispatch. Other RECAP members are involved in similar efforts. They meet regularly to discuss technique and review their progress.

I'm not sure how I feel about all this. I'm a middle-age white guy, which means I'm constantly reminded that my particular group is responsible for the oppression of every known minority PLUS most wars PLUS government corruption PLUS pollution of the environment, not to mention that it was middle-age white guys who killed Bambi's mom. So I'm pleased to learn that I myself am an oppressed victim of something. But no matter how hard I try, I can't get enraged about it. I've asked other guys about this.

"Are you enraged about being circumcised?" I say.

"What?" they say.

So I explain about RECAP.

"WHAT??" they say.

I have yet to find a guy who's enraged. And nobody I talked to was interested in miniature barbells, let alone surgery. Most guys don't even like to *talk* about medical procedures involving the Oregonian region. One time my wife and I were at a restaurant with two other couples, and one of the women, Susan, started describing her husband Bob's vasectomy, which she had witnessed.

"NO!" we guys shouted, curling our bodies up like boiled shrimp. "Let's not talk about that!"

But our wives were *fascinated*. They egged Susan on, and she went into great detail, forcing us guys to stick wads of French bread in our ears and duck our heads under the table. Periodically, we'd come up to see if the coast was clear, but Susan would be saying, "And then the doctor picked up this thing that looked like a big crochet needle . . ." And *BONK* we guys would bang our heads together ducking back under the table.

So Post-Dispatchwise, I think I'm going to remain an oppressed victim. But don't let me tell the rest of you guys what to think; it's your decision. This is a free country. In most communities.

TARTS AFIRE

The thing I like best about being a journalist, aside from being able to clip my toenails while working, is that sometimes, through hard work and perseverance and opening my mail, I come across a story that can really help you, the consumer, gain a better understanding of how you can be killed by breakfast snack food.

This is just such a time. I have received, from alert reader Richard Rilke, an alarming article from the *New Philadelphia* (Ohio) *Times-Reporter* headlined: OVERHEATED POP-TARTS CAUSE DOVER HOUSE FIRE, OFFICIALS SAY. The article states that fire officials investigating a house fire in Dover, Ohio, concluded that "when the toaster failed to eject the Pop-Tarts, they caught fire and set the kitchen ablaze."

According to the article, the investigators reached this conclusion after experimenting with Pop-Tarts and a toaster. They found that "strawberry Pop-Tarts, when left in a toaster that doesn't pop up, will send flames 'like a blowtorch' up to three feet high."

Like most Americans, I have long had a keen scientific interest in combustible breakfast foods, so I called up the

TART WARS

Dover Fire Department and spoke to investigator Don Dunfee. He told me that he and some other investigators bought a used toaster, rigged it so it wouldn't pop up, put in some Kellogg's strawberry Pop-Tarts, then observed the results.

"At five minutes and 55 seconds," he said, "we had flames shooting out the top. I mean *large* flames. We also tried it with an off-brand tart. That one broke into flames in like 3½ minutes, but it wasn't near as impressive as the Kellogg's Pop-Tart."

A quality you will find in top investigative journalists such as Woodward and Bernstein and myself is that before we publish a sensational story, we make every effort to verify the facts, unless this would be boring. So after speaking with Dunfee I proceeded to my local Kmart, where I consulted with an employee in the appliance sector.

ME: What kind of toaster do you recommend for outdoor use?

EMPLOYEE: A cheap toaster.

I got one for $8.96. I already had Kellogg's strawberry Pop-Tarts at home, because these are one of the three major food groups that my son eats, the other two being (1) pizza and (2) pizza with pepperoni.

Having assembled the equipment, I was ready to conduct the experiment.

WARNING: DO NOT ATTEMPT THE FOLLOWING EXPERIMENT YOURSELF. THIS IS A DANGEROUS EXPERIMENT CONDUCTED BY A TRAINED HUMOR COLUMNIST UNDER CAREFULLY CONTROLLED CONDITIONS, NAMELY, HIS WIFE WAS NOT HOME.

I conducted the experiment on a Saturday night. Assisting me was my neighbor, Steele Reeder, who is a Customs broker, which I believe is a mentally stressful occupation, because when I mentioned the experiment to Steele he became very excited, ran home, and came back wearing (this is true) a bright yellow rubber rain suit, an enormous sun hat, and a rope around his waist holding a fire extinguisher on each hip, gunslinger-style. He also carried a first-aid kit containing, among other things, the largest tube of Preparation H that I have ever seen.

Also on hand was Steele's wife, Bobette, who pointed out that we had become pathetic old people, inasmuch as our Saturday Night Action now consisted of hoping to see a toaster fire.

Using an extension cord, we set the toaster up a safe distance away from the house. I then inserted two Kellogg's strawberry Pop-Tarts ("With Smucker's Real

Fruit'') and Steele, wearing thick gloves, held the toaster lever down so it couldn't pop up. After about two minutes the toaster started to make a desperate rattling sound, which is how toasters in the wild signal to the rest of the herd that they are in distress. A minute later the Pop-Tarts started smoking, and at 5 minutes and 50 seconds, scary flames began shooting up 20 to 30 inches out of both toaster slots. It was a dramatic moment, very similar to the one that occurred in the New Mexico desert nearly 50 years ago, when the awestruck atomic scientists of the Manhattan Project witnessed the massive blast that erupted from their first crude experimental snack pastry.

We unplugged the extension cord, extinguished the blaze, and determined that the toaster's career as a professional small appliance was over. It was time to draw conclusions. The obvious one involves missile defense. As you are aware, President Clinton has decided to cut way back on Star Wars research, so that there will be more money available for pressing domestic needs, such as creating jobs and keeping airport runways clear for urgent presidential grooming. But by using currently available electronic and baking technology, we could build giant toasters and place them around the U.S., then load them with enormous Pop-Tarts. When we detected incoming missiles, we'd simply hold the toaster levers down via some method (possibly involving Tom and Roseanne Arnold) and within a few minutes *WHOOM* the country would be surrounded by a protective wall of flames, and the missiles would either burn up or get knocked off course and detonate harmlessly in some place like New Jersey.

Anyway, that's what I think we should do, and if you think the same thing, then you have inhaled *way* too many Smucker's fumes.

INSECT ASIDE

Recently, I had to pay several hundred dollars to get my car started, and do you want to know why? Nature, that's why. It's getting out of control.

Now before I get a lot of angry mail on recycled paper, let me stress that, generally, I'm in favor of nature. I'm even in favor of scary nature, such as snakes, because I know that snakes play a vital role in the ecosystem (specifically, the role of Boonga the Demon Creature).

But nature should stay in its proper context. For example, the proper context for snakes is Asia. A snake should not be in your yard unless it has your written permission. A snake should *definitely* not be climbing your trees, although this is exactly what one was doing outside my window a few days ago. I looked out and there it was, going straight up the trunk, looking casual, Mr. Cool-Blooded. It was impressive. I'm always amazed that snakes can move on the *ground,* without arms or legs. You try lying on your stomach and moving forward merely by writhing. My friend Buzz Burger did this for an hour at the MacPhersons' 1977 New Year's Eve party and never got out of the kitchen.

Nevertheless I was alarmed to see the snake, because according to top snake scientists, there's only one known scientific reason why a snake would go up a tree, namely, so it can leap onto your head and strangle you.

This particular snake had been watching me for several days. I'd seen it on the lawn earlier when I was out with my two dogs, Earnest and Zippy, who were trotting in front, looking alert and vigilant, providing protection. The snake was holding very still, which is a ploy that a snake will use to fool the observer into thinking that it's a harmless object, such as a garden hose or a snake made out of rubber. This ploy is effective only if the observer has the IQ of a breath mint, so it worked perfectly on my dogs, who vigilantly trotted right past the snake. Earnest actually stepped *over* part of the snake.

Of course, if the snake had been something harmless, the dogs would have spotted it instantly. Zippy, for example, goes into a violent barking rage whenever he notices the swimming-pool chlorine dispenser. This is a small, benign plastic object that floats in the pool and has never made a hostile move in its life. But Zippy is convinced that it's a malignant entity, just waiting for the right moment to lunge out of the water, *Jaws*-like, and dispense lethal doses of chlorine all over its helpless victims.

I tried to notify the dogs about the snake. "Look!" I said, pointing. "A snake!" This caused the dogs to alertly trot over and sniff my finger in case there was peanut butter on it. The snake, continuing to hold still, was watching all this, thinking: "This person will be *easy* to strangle."

So now I find myself glancing up nervously whenever I walk across my yard. I'm thinking maybe I should carry an open umbrella at all times, as a Snake Deflector. But that is not my point. By now you have forgotten my point, which involves my car. One day it wouldn't start, and it had to be towed to our garage, which has two main characters: Bill, who is responsible for working on the car; and Sal, who is responsible for giving you a dramatic account of what was wrong.

"At first we thought it was the (something)," Sal told me, when it was all over. "But when we tried to (something) the (something), all we got was (something)! Can you believe it?"

"No," I assured him.

"So then," said Sal, starting to gesture, "we tested the (something), but . . ."

He continued for 10 minutes, attracting a small but appreciative audience. Finally, he reached the crucial dramatic moment, where Bill had narrowed the problem down to a key car part, called the "something." Carefully,

Bill removed this part. Slowly, he opened it up. And there, inside, he found: ants.

Yes. An ant squadron was living in my car part and *eating the wires*. I am not making this up.

"Oh, yes," said Sal. "Ants will eat your wires."

This gave me a terrible feeling of what the French call *déjà vu,* meaning "big insect trouble." Because just a month earlier, the water in our house stopped running, and a paid professional plumber came out and informed us that—I am still not making this up—there were *ants in our pump switch.*

This is what I mean by nature getting out of hand. It's not *natural* for ants to eat car and pump parts. Ants should eat the foods provided by the ecosystem, such as dropped Milk Duds. Something is wrong.

And here's another scary but absolutely true fact: Lately I've noticed ants going into the paper slot of *my computer's laser printer.* Ask yourself: What natural business would ants have with a laser? You can bet that whatever they're up to, it's not going to benefit mankind, not after all the stuff *we've* sprayed on them.

So I'm worried. I'm worried in my car; I'm worried in my house; and above all I'm worried when I cross my yard. I'm afraid that one day I'll disappear, and the police will search my property, and all they'll find will be a snake who obviously just ate a large meal and is pretending to be a really fat garden hose; and maybe some glowing ants munching on, say, the microwave oven; and of course Zippy, Mr. Vigilant, barking at the chlorine dispenser.

INVASION OF THE
MONEY SNATCHERS

Sometimes, even though we love America, with its amber waves of purple mounted majesties fruiting all over the plains, we get a little ticked off at our government. Sometimes we find ourselves muttering: "All the government ever seems to do is suck up our hard-earned money and spew it out on projects such as the V-22 Osprey military aircraft, which the Pentagon doesn't even *want,* and which tends to crash, but which Congress has fought to spend millions on, anyway, because this will help the reelection efforts of certain congresspersons, who would cheerfully vote to spend millions on a program to develop a working artificial hemorrhoid, as long as the money would be spent in their districts."

I mutter this frequently myself. But we must not allow ourselves to become cynical. We must remember that for every instance of the government's demonstrating the intelligence of a yam, there is also an instance of the government's rising to the level of a far more complex vegetable, such as the turnip.

Today I'm pleased to tell you the heartwarming story of

a group of 10 men whose lives have been changed, thanks to prompt, coordinated government action. I got this story from one of the men, Al Oliver, a retired Navy chaplain. In fact, all 10 are retirees (or, in Al Oliver's words, "chronologically disadvantaged").

The men live in the Azalea Trace retirement center in Pensacola, Florida. For years they've gathered every morning to drink coffee and talk. In 1988, they formed a pact: Each would buy a Florida lottery ticket every week, and if anybody won, they'd all split the money. They called themselves the Lavender Hill Mob, and stamped that name on their lottery tickets.

For three years they won nothing. Then, in 1991, one of

their tickets had five out of six winning numbers, for a prize of $4,156. Oliver took the ticket to the state lottery office in Pensacola, where he had to fill out Form 5754, indicating who was to get the money. He wrote down "Lavender Hill Mob."

A while later, he got the form back from the state, along with a letter informing him that the Lavender Hill Mob was a partnership and could not be paid until it obtained an Employer Identification Number, or EIN, from (*ominous music starts here*) ... the Internal Revenue Service.

At this point you readers are like an audience watching the scene in a horror movie wherein the woman trapped alone in the house at night is about to go down into the basement.

"NO! NO!" you're shouting to Al Oliver. "Don't get involved with the IRS! Better to just throw the ticket away!"

But Oliver went to an IRS office and applied for the EIN by filling out Form SS-4. "I had to list everything on all 10 of us except I believe our cholesterol count," he recalls. The IRS then gave him the EIN, which he sent along with Form 5754 to the state lottery, which sent him the check, which he took to the bank, which, after balking a little, finally gave him 10 cashier's checks for the Lavender Hill Mob members.

Now you're thinking: "OK, so it was an annoying bureaucratic hassle, but everything turned out fine."

Please try not to be such a wienerhead. Of COURSE everything did not turn out fine. In February, Oliver began receiving notices from the IRS demanding to know where exactly the hell were the Lavender Hill Mob's 1065 forms showing partnership income for 1989, 1990, and 1991. So Oliver went to his CPA, who filled out the forms with zeros and sent them in.

73

Of course this only angered the IRS, because here the Lavender Hill Mob was just now getting around to filing forms for as far back as 1989, which means these forms were LATE. You can't allow that kind of flagrant disregard for the law. You let the Mob members slide on that, and the next thing you know they're selling crack on the shuffleboard court.

So in June the IRS notified the Mob members that, for failing to file their 1989 Form 1065 on time, they owed a penalty of $2,500. Oliver's CPA, who is not working for free, wrote a letter to the IRS attempting to explain everything. Then in July the Mobsters got another notice, informing them that they owed $2,500 PLUS $19.20 in interest charges, which will of course continue to mount. The notice states that the government may file a tax lien against the Mobsters and adds: "WE MUST ALSO CONSIDER TAKING YOUR WAGES, PROPERTY OR OTHER ASSETS."

That's where it stood when I last heard from Oliver. Since this whole thing is obviously a simple misunderstanding, we can safely assume that it will never be resolved. The wisest course for the Mobsters would be to turn all their worldly goods over to the government right now. Because if they keep attempting to file the correct form, they're going to wind up in serious trouble, fleeing through the swamps around Pensacola, pursued by airborne IRS agents in the new V-22 Osprey, suspended via steel cables from some aircraft that can actually fly.

READER ALERT

This next section is more or less about travel-ing. It includes an account of my visit to Com-munist China, where I spent almost an entire day, thereby qualifying as an authority.

There's also a column I wrote about people who are obnoxious on airplanes. This column was *very* popular with flight attendants; for quite a while after it was published, whenever I'd take a plane, the attendants would give me free beers. That's why I got into journalism in the first place: to help people.

HELL ON WINGS

I'm in an airplane, strapped into my seat, no way to escape. For an hour we've been taxiing around Miami International Airport while lightning tries to hit us. Earlier I was hoping that the plane might at some point actually take off and fly to our intended destination, but now I'm starting to root for the lightning, because a direct strike might silence the two women sitting in front of me. There's only one empty seat between them, but they're speaking at a decibel level that would be appropriate if one of them were in Cleveland. Also, they both have Blitherers Disease, which occurs when there is no filter attached to the brain, so that every thought the victim has, no matter how minor, comes blurting right out. This means that the rest of us passengers are being treated to repartee such as this:

FIRST WOMAN: I PREFER A WINDOW SEAT.

SECOND WOMAN: OH, NOT ME. I ALWAYS PREFER AN AISLE SEAT.

FIRST WOMAN: THAT'S JUST LIKE MY SON. HE LIVES IN NEW JERSEY, AND HE ALWAYS PREFERS AN AISLE SEAT ALSO.

SECOND WOMAN: MY SISTER-IN-LAW WORKS FOR A DENTIST IN NEW JERSEY. HE'S AN EXCELLENT DENTIST BUT HE CAN'T PRONOUNCE HIS *R*'S. HE SAYS, "I'M AFWAID YOU NEED A WOOT CANAL."

FIRST WOMAN: MY BROTHER-IN-LAW JUST HAD THAT ROOT CANAL. HE WAS BLEEDING ALL OVER HIS NEW CAR, ONE OF THOSE JAPANESE ONES, A WHADDYACALLEM, LEXIT.

SECOND WOMAN: I PREFER A BUICK, BUT LET ME TELL YOU, THIS INSURANCE, WHO CAN AFFORD IT?

FIRST WOMAN: I HAVE A BROTHER IN THE INSURANCE BUSINESS, WITH ANGINA. HE PREFERS A WINDOW SEAT.

SECOND WOMAN: OH, NOT ME. I ALWAYS PREFER AN AISLE. NOW MY DAUGHTER . . .

And so it has gone, for one solid hour, a live broadcast of random neural firings. The harder I try to ignore it, the more my brain focuses on it. But it could be worse. I could be the flight attendant. Every time she walks past the two women, they both shout "MISS?" It's an uncontrollable reflex.

"MISS?" they are shouting. "CAN WE GET A BEVERAGE HERE?" This is maybe the fifth time they have asked this.

"I'm sorry," says the flight attendant, with incredible patience. "We can't serve any beverages until after we take off."

This answer never satisfies the women, who do not seem to be fully aware of the fact that the plane is still on the ground. They've decided that the flight attendant has a bad attitude. As she moves away, they discuss this in what they apparently believe is a whisper.

"SHE'S VERY RUDE," they say, their voices booming through the cabin, possibly audible in other planes. "THEY SHOULD FIRE HER." "YES, THEY SHOULD."

77

"THERE'S SUPPOSED TO BE BEVERAGE SERVICE."
"MISS??"

It's a good thing for society in general that I'm not a flight attendant, because I would definitely kill somebody no later than my second day. Recently, I sat on a bumpy, crowded flight and watched a 40-ish flight attendant, both arms occupied with a large stack of used dinner trays, struggling down the aisle, trying to maintain her balance, and a young man held out his coffee cup, *blocking her path*, and in a loud, irritated voice said, quote: "Hon? Can I get a refill? Like maybe today?"

Hon.

She smiled—not with her eyes—and said, "I'll be with you as soon as I can, sir."

Sir.

Oh, I'd be with him soon, all right. I'd come up behind him and strangle him with the movie-headphone cord. "Is that tight enough for you, *sir?*" would be the last words he'd ever hear. Then I'd become a legendary outlaw flight attendant. I'd hide in the overhead luggage compartment and watch for problems, such as people flying with small children and making no effort to control them, people who think it's *cute* when their children shriek and pour salad dressing onto other passengers. When this happened *BANG* the luggage compartment would burst open and out would leap: the Avenging Flight Attendant of Doom, his secret identity concealed by a mask made from a barf bag with holes in it. He'd snatch the child and say to the parents, very politely, "I'm sorry, but FAA regulations require me to have this child raised by somebody more civilized, such as wolves." If they tried to stop him, he'd pin them in their seats with dense, 200-pound airline omelets.

Insane? Yes, I'm insane, and you would be, too, if you were listening to these two women.

"MISS??" they are saying. "IT'S TOO HOT IN HERE." "CAN WE GET SOME BEVERAGE SERVICE?" "MISS???"

And now the pilot is making an announcement. "Well, folks" is how he starts. This is a bad sign. They always start with "Well, folks" when they're going to announce something bad, as in: "Well, folks, if we dump the fuel, we might be able to glide as far as the mainland."

This time the pilot announces that—I swear I am not making this up—*lightning has struck the control tower.*

"We could be sitting here for some time," he says.

"MISS????" say the women in front of me.

No problem. I can handle it. I'll just stay calm, reach into the seat pocket, very slowly pull out the headphone cord . . .

THE GREAT MALL OF CHINA

The World's Great Capitalists Market to the Old Butchers Who Run China. They've Promised to Be Nice.

If you listen hard, as you wander around Hong Kong, you can almost hear the clock.

Tick tick tick tick tick, it says, over the rushed city sounds of the traffic, the boats, the people.

Tick tick tick tick tick . . .

Get ready. It's coming.

Midnight, June 30, 1997. This will be a very big day for Hong Kong. The biggest ever. Hotel space is already selling out. A lot of people want to be there, to remember what Hong Kong was, to get a glimpse of what it will be.

Then the sightseers will check out and go home, leaving Hong Kong to face . . . whatever comes next. Nobody knows for sure what it will be. But it's coming.

Tick tick tick tick tick . . .

Some background. Although Hong Kong is geographically part of China, right now it's a colony of Great Britain. This arrangement dates back to the 19th-century Opium Wars, which you recall from your high school World History class.

You liar. Probably the only event you remember from

World History class is the time Jeffrey Brunderman made
a spitball so large that he couldn't get it out of his mouth
without emergency medical assistance. To refresh your
memory: In the early 19th century, British traders were
making big money getting opium from India and selling
it, illegally, in China. In 1839, the Chinese emperor tried
to put a stop to this. Britain, which at the time had a vast
empire and a major butt-kicking navy, was outraged that
some pissant emperor would dare to interfere with the

activities of legitimate British businessmen just because they were smuggling drugs.

So Britain sent a fleet to attack. The Chinese were quickly defeated and forced to sign a treaty under which, among other things, Britain got Hong Kong. Over the years Britain added more land to the Hong Kong colony, which is ruled by a governor appointed by the crown. Historically, the Hong Kong residents, who are overwhelmingly Chinese, have had virtually no say in their government.

But for a long time Hong Kong didn't concern itself much with politics, because there was a lot of money to be made. There still is. Hong Kong today is a major international trade and financial center. It's a busy place—410 square miles supporting six million people, most of them jammed together around the spectacular, hardworking Hong Kong harbor, which we travel writers are required, by law, to describe as "teeming."

And it is teeming. All day, all night, the dirty brown water is churned by boats, all sizes and shapes, barely missing each other as they bustle in all directions on urgent boat errands. Many are ferryboats, which cross the harbor constantly, carrying the teeming masses of people—mostly well-dressed, prosperous-looking people—to and from the downtown business district, which looks like a full-size version of an Epcot Center scale model of the City of Tomorrow: dozens of breathtakingly tall, shiny, modernistic buildings, none of which appears to be more than a few days old, with newer ones constantly going up. Connecting these buildings, over the teeming streets, are teeming walkways, which lead to vast, staggeringly opulent shopping centers with gleaming floors and spotless stores teeming with cameras, electronics, silks, jewelry, and other luxury items of all kinds.

This is not a place for quiet reflection. This is the Ultimate Shopping Mall. This is a place where everything is for sale, and you can bargain your brains out. This is a place where you can feel your credit cards teeming in your wallet, hear their squeaky little plastic voices calling, "Let us out! Let us OUT!!" This is a place so rich and modern and fast-paced and sophisticated that it makes New York seem like a dowdy old snooze of a town.

In short, this is a place that screams: "We're RICH, SUCCESSFUL CAPITALISTS, and we're DAMNED PROUD OF IT!"

And on June 30, 1997, Britain is going to give it all—the whole marvelous money machine, and all its human dependents—to the People's Republic of China. China has long claimed that Britain has no right to Hong Kong, and in 1984, after much negotiation between the two nations, Britain agreed to get out in 1997.

So in a little over five years, the people of Hong Kong—who never got to vote on any of this—will simply be handed over to China, as though they were some kind of commodity, nothing but a load of pork bellies being traded. The Chinese leaders have promised that they won't make any drastic changes in Hong Kong, but nobody believes this. These are, after all, the same fun dudes who gave us the Tiananmen Square massacre.

Tick tick tick tick tick . . .

So today Hong Kong is nervous. People with money or connections are fleeing by the thousands. But millions more can't leave, or don't want to abandon their homeland. They're staying, and waiting. Nobody is sure what's coming, but it's definitely coming. Five years. About 2,000 days, and counting. This knowledge hangs over Hong Kong like a fog, giving the city an edgy, quietly desperate, *Casablanca*-like feel.

Tick tick tick tick tick . . .

Or maybe not. Maybe my imagination was just hyperactive from drinking San Miguel beer on a moody gray day and watching the harbor being whipped into whitecaps by a typhoon named—really—Fred. The truth is that, most of the time, daily Hong Kong life seemed pretty normal. People were teeming and working and shopping and eating and laughing just the way people would if they weren't doomed to be turned over to a group of hard-eyed old murderers.

While my family and I were there, in August, the big news story, aside from Typhoon Fred, was the trial of Hong Kong businessman Chin Chi-ming, accused of blackmailing actresses into having sex with him. The Hong Kong media was covering the heck out of this trial. Here's an excerpt from the *South China Morning Post* story concerning a witness identified as "Mrs. D" being cross-examined by defense attorney Kevin Egan:

Mr. Egan started by asking Mrs. D if she had noticed whether Chin's organ was erect while they were in bed. The witness said it was.

Mr. Egan then asked if it was "fully" erect, but prosecutor, Mr. Stuart Cotsen, objected to the question on the grounds that the witness could not be expected to know.

Mr. Egan said the objection meant he had to ask the witness to describe Chin's sexual organ as fully as possible.

So apparently life goes on in Hong Kong. I highly recommend it as a travel destination, at least until 1997, although you may feel a little intimidated by the crowds until you learn how to teem. You have to get your elbows into it. I learned this one afternoon when we decided to take a ferry to Macao, which is the other non-Communist territory in China, about 40 miles west of Hong Kong. Macao is an old colony belonging to Portugal, which will turn it over to China in 1999. Gambling is legal in Macao, and a lot of Hong Kong residents regularly teem over there on ferries and go to the casinos.

One day we went over, and when our ferry landed, the other passengers tried to kill us. OK, technically they weren't *trying* to kill us; they were trying to be first in line to get through Immigration and Customs. But they did not hesitate to shove us violently out of the way. We were bouncing around like kernels in a popcorn maker and quickly became separated. Occasionally, through the crowd, I'd see my wife and son, expressions of terror on their faces, being jostled off in the general direction of the Philippines.

I tried being polite. "Hey!" I said to a middle-age, polite-looking man behind me who was thoughtfully attempting to hasten my progress by jabbing me repeatedly in the spine with his umbrella tip. "Excuse me! I SAID EXCUSE ME, DAMMIT!!"

But we quickly learned that the only way to function in these crowds was to teem right along with everybody else. When it came time to purchase return ferry tickets, I was practically a professional. I got into the "line," which was a formless, milling mass of people, and I leaned hard in the general direction of the ticket window. I finally got close to it, and it was clearly my turn to go next, when an old man—he had to be at least 75—started making a strong move around me from my left. I had a definite age and size advantage, but this man was good. He shoved his right elbow deep into my gut while he reached his left arm out to grasp the ticket window ledge. I leaned hard on the man sideways, and then—

you can't teach this kind of thing; you have to have an instinct for it—I made a beautiful counterclockwise spin move that got me to the window inches ahead of him. I stuck my face smack up against the window, confident I had won, but then the old man, showing great resourcefulness, stuck his head under my arm and shoved his face into the window, too. We were cheek to cheek, faces against the glass, mouths gaping and eyes bulging like two crazed carp, shouting ticket orders. Unfortunately, he was shouting in Chinese, which gave him the advantage, and he got his ticket first. But I was definitely making progress.

However, I never really did adjust to Chinese food. I have always loved Chinese food the way they make it here in the U.S., where you order from an English menu and the dishes have reassuring names such as "sweet and sour pork" and you never see what the food looked like before it was killed and disassembled. This is not the kind of Chinese food that actual Chinese people eat. For one thing, before they order something at a restaurant, they like to see the prospective entrée demonstrate its physical fitness by swimming or walking around.

One day we were wandering through the narrow, zigzagging (and of course teeming) side streets of Macao, and we came to a group of small stalls and shops; in front of each one were stacks of big glass tanks containing murky water filled with squirming populations of fish, eels, squids, turtles, etc. At first we thought we'd entered the Aquarium Supplies District, but then we saw tables behind the tanks, and we realized that these were all *restaurants*. People were *eating* these things. You, the diner, would select the eel that you felt best exemplified whatever qualities are considered desirable in an eel, such as a nice, even coating of slime, and the restaurant owner would haul it out of the tank so you could take a closer look, and if it met with your approval—*WHACK*—dinner would be served.

We walked by one restaurant just as a man reached into a tank and hauled out what looked like the world's biggest newt. It had legs and a tail and buggy eyes, and I swear it was the size of a small dog. The man displayed it to some diners, who looked at this *thing*, thrashing around inches from their faces, and instead of sprinting to a safe distance, as I definitely would have, they were *nodding thoughtfully*, the way you might approve a bottle of Chablis.

A few minutes later, we came to a larger restaurant that had an elaborate window display, with colored spotlights shining on an arrangement of strange, triangular, withered, vaguely evil-looking things.

"Shark fins," said my wife, who reads all the guidebooks. "They're very popular."

At least they were dead. Around the corner we found another restaurant window display, consisting of a jar full of—I am not making this up—*snakes*.

"Come on in!" was the basic message of this display. "Have some snake!"

So as you can imagine we were a tad reluctant to eat local cuisine. But one night in Hong Kong we decided to give it a try, and we asked a bouncer outside a bar to recommend a medium-priced Chinese restaurant. He directed us down a side street to a little open-air place decorated in a design motif that I would call "about six old card tables." Several men were eating out of bowls. We sat down, and the waitress, a jolly woman who seemed vastly amused by our presence, rooted around and found a beat-up hand-written English menu for us. Here are some of the entrées it listed:

Ox Offal and Noodle
Sea Blubber
Sliced Cuttle Fish
Sliced Pork's Skin
Pig's Trotters
Clam's Meat
Goose's Intestines
Preserved Pig's Blood

Using our fluent gesturing skills, we communicated that we wanted chicken, beef, and pork, but definitely *not* Preserved Pig's Blood. We also ordered a couple of beers, which the waitress brought out still attached to the plastic six-pack holder. Our food arrived maybe a minute later, and the waitress stayed to watch us eat it. Several of the other diners also got up and gathered around, laughing and gesturing. We were big entertainment.

My dish, which was probably pork, tasted pretty good. My son refused to eat his dish, which I would describe as "chicken parts not really cooked." My wife's dish was apparently the beef; she said it was OK, although it was very spicy and caused her nose to run. There were no napkins, but the restaurant did provide a tabletop roll of toilet paper in a nice ceramic dispenser, which we thought was a classy touch. The whole meal, including a generous tip, cost about eight U.S. dollars. We were glad we hadn't asked the bouncer to recommend an *inexpensive* restaurant.

I should stress here that Hong Kong is famous for fine dining, and has a mind-boggling array of restaurants offering a vast variety of cuisines, including many that even provincial wussies like ourselves can eat. I should also stress that there are other things to do in Hong Kong besides eat and shop. You can ride the ferries, which are cheap and romantic and exciting. You can teem around the streets and pretend that you are some kind of slick international businessperson. You can take a tram that seems to go straight up the side of a mountain—in the old days, Chinese servants used to carry their British masters up this mountain on sedan chairs—and look down on an indescribably glorious view of the city and harbor, and be moved to say, in unison with 350 other tourists, "Look at that VIEW!" And you can take a day trip to the People's Republic of China, future landlords of Hong Kong. We took such a trip. Here's how it went:

HONG KONG, 7 A.M.

The tour-company bus picks us up at our hotel early on a day that promises to be rainy and blustery, thanks to the tail end of Typhoon Fred. We're each given a sticker to wear on our clothing; it has the name of the tour company and the words "IF NOT PICKED, CALL 5-445656." At various other hotels we gather the rest of our group, about 20 people from the U.S., Australia, and England. We're taken to a ferry terminal, where we stand next to a sign that says BEWARE YOUR OWN PROPERTY, waiting for our guide.

"Don't lose your sticker," an American man is saying to his family. "If you lose your sticker, you have to stay in China." This is of course a joke, we hope.

Finally, our guide arrives—a very tall, thin, easygoing young Hong Kong man who says we should call him Tommy. (We found that guides identified themselves to us by Western nicknames, on the assumption, no doubt correct, that we'd have trouble pronouncing their real names.) Tommy briefs us on our itinerary.

"Because we have only one day to see China, maybe our tour will be a little bit rushed," he points out.

After an hour's ride on a hydrofoil ferry, we arrive in the People's Republic at a city called Shekou, which

Tommy tells us means "mouth of the snake." We line up to go through Immigration and Customs, next to signs warning us not to try to bring in any hot peppers or eggplants. I personally would not dream of attempting such a thing. God knows what this country does to eggplant smugglers.

Next to the Immigration area is a counter where you can buy duty-free cognac and American cigarettes. This strikes us as a pretty decadent enterprise for the People's Republic to be engaging in.

Outside Customs Tommy introduces us to another guide, John, who'll be escorting us around the People's Republic in an aging bus driven by Bill. John is an earnest young man who possesses many facts about the People's Republic and an uncontrollable urge to repeat them. He tells us that our first stop is a museum where we'll see the World Famous Terra Cotta Warriors and Horses, which have been called—at least 20 times in our tour bus alone— "The Eighth Wonder of the World." These are life-size clay statues of horses and warriors; 8,000 of these statues were buried with a Chinese emperor in 221 B.C., to protect him. This was before the invention of burglar alarms.

A few dozen statues have been placed on display in the Shekou museum, which is actually the second floor of a commercial-type building. On the first floor is a store that sells industrial equipment; the window has a nice display entitled "Compressed Air Breathing Apparatus."

The museum itself, in terms of space allocation, is about 25 percent exhibit and 75 percent gift shops. Aside from our group, the only visitors are sticker-wearing tourists from other tour buses. We look briefly at the exhibit of World Famous Terra Cotta Warriors and Horses, then browse through a half-dozen shops selling jewelry, silks, jade, souvenirs, postcards, and other authentic cultural items. Your major credit cards are more than welcome here in the People's Republic.

Back on the bus, John informs us, over and over, that Shekou is part of a Special Economic Zone that the People's Republic has set up to encourage economic development. The relatively few Chinese who are lucky enough to live inside the Special Economic Zone, he says, are allowed to engage in all kinds of wild and crazy economic activities such as actually choosing their own jobs and maybe even own small businesses—in short, they're totally free to do just about anything except say or do the wrong thing, in which case they'll be run over by tanks. (John doesn't state this last part explicitly.)

John also discusses the plan for the "recovery" of Hong Kong in 1997.

"Hong Kong will enjoy a high degree of autonomous," he assures us.

Our next stop is what John calls the "free market," which turns out to be a line of about 25 fruit vendors who are aiding in the development of the Chinese economy by selling apples and pears to busloads of sticker-wearing tourists for what I suspect is 10 times the local price. We dutifully file off the bus in a pelting rain and walk over to the vendors, who are attracting us via the marketing technique of waving pieces of fruit and shouting "Hello!" Being a savvy free-market Westerner, I am able, using shrewd bargaining techniques, to purchase an apple for what I later calculate is two American dollars.

Back on the bus, John starts reviewing the concept of the Special Economic Zone for the benefit of those who missed it the first five or six times. This gives me an opportunity to stare out the window in terror at the traffic. China has achieved a totally free-market traffic system, as far as I can tell. There are virtually no traffic lights, and apparently anybody is allowed to drive anywhere, in any direction. Everybody is constantly barging in front of everybody else, missing each other by molecules. The only law seems to be that if your horn works, you have to provide clear audible proof of this at least once every 30 seconds.

If you didn't know that Shekou was a Special Economic Zone, you probably wouldn't be very impressed by it. The buildings are mostly grim, industrial, and dirty; many seem to be crumbling. The roads are uneven, sometimes dirt, always potholed. But this area is turning into a manufacturing monster. Encouraged by the Chinese government, many foreign companies have located factories here, and China now exports more than $60 billion worth of goods a year. The United States buys a quarter of this, all kinds of items, including a tenth of our shoes and a third of our toys. They are big-time, Most-Favored-Nation trading partners of ours, the Chinese.

Our tour does not include a manufacturing stop. Instead we go to what John says is the largest kindergarten in Shekou, where we're going to see the children put on a show. We arrive just as another group of sticker-wearers is leaving. We sit on tiny chairs, and a dozen heartrendingly cute children, even cuter than the animated figures in the It's a Small World After All boat ride, play instruments and dance for us while we take pictures like crazy. Fond memories of the People's Republic.

As we leave, we learn that school isn't actually in session; the children are here just to entertain the tourists.

Getting back on the bus, my son has an insight.

"Really," he says, "all kids are in a communism country, because they have to obey orders and they get pushed around."

I agree that this is true, but he will still have to take out the garbage.

Now John is telling us how this city came to be called "the mouth of the snake." It's a long, old legend involving a snake that came here on a rainy day and turned into a beautiful woman (why not?), and a man lent her his umbrella, and they fell in love, and then needless to say this attracted the attention of the Underwater Dragon King. It's a very complex legend, and I hope there isn't going to be a quiz.

Outside the window we see a large group of dogs, all tethered to a post, looking around with the standard earnest, vaguely cheerful dog expression. Some men are looking the dogs over, the way supermarket shoppers look over tomatoes. John is back on the endlessly fascinating topic of the Special Economic Zone, telling us how many square kilometers it is. This is not what I'm wondering about. What I'm wondering is: Are they going to *eat* those dogs? But I don't ask, because I don't really want to know.

Now we're going through a security checkpoint, leaving the Special Economic Zone and its many freedoms. Now we're in the real People's Republic, which makes the Special Economic Zone look like Epcot Center. Everywhere there are half-finished buildings, seemingly abandoned years ago in midconstruction, some of them with laundry hanging in them. There are also people everywhere, but nobody seems to be *doing* anything. I admit this is purely an impression, but it's a strong one. The primary activities seem to be:

1. Seeing how many bundles you can pile on a bicycle and still ride it, and
2. Sitting around.

We go through a line of tollbooths—our booth was manned by six people—and get on an extremely surreal expressway. Picture a major, semimodern, four-lane, interstate-type highway, except that it has every kind of

93

vehicle—mostly older trucks and buses, but also motorcycles, tractors, bicycles with bundles piled incredibly high, even hand-drawn carts. Also you come across the occasional water buffalo, wandering along. Yes! Water buffalo! On the interstate! Bear in mind that this is the *industrially advanced* region of China.

Of course, all the vehicles, including the water buffalo, freely use both lanes. So our bus is constantly weaving and honking, accelerating to a top speed of about 45 miles per hour, then suddenly dropping to zero. We pass a truck with a flat tire; somebody has removed the wheel and thoughtfully left it in the traffic lane. We pass an overturned pig truck, with the pigs still in it, looking concerned. A group of people has gathered to sit around and watch. We pass two more overturned trucks, each of which has also attracted a seated audience. Maybe at some point the trucks here just spontaneously leap up and right themselves, and nobody wants to miss it.

All the while, John is talking about square kilometers and metric tons, but we tourists are not paying attention. We're staring out the window, fascinated by the highway drama.

After about an hour we arrive in Dongguang, where we're going to stop for lunch.

"People here like to eat poisonous snakes," John informs us. This makes me nervous about what we're having for lunch, especially after the scene with the dogs. Plus, I can't help thinking about an alarming development in Chinese cuisine that I read about a few days earlier in a newspaper story, which I will quote from here:

Beijing (AP)—Health officials closed down 92 restaurants in a single city (Luoyang) for putting opium poppy pods in food served to customers, an official newspaper has reported . . . in an attempt to get customers addicted to their food . . . health officials started getting suspicious when they saw that some noodle shops and food stalls were attracting long lines of customers while others nearby did little business.

So I'm concerned that they're going to offer us some delicacy whose name translates to "Poodle and Viper Stew with 'Can't Say No' Noodles." I'm relieved when John tells us we're having Peking Duck. We pull up to a hotel and enter the dining room, where, lo and behold, we find that we'll be dining with the very same sticker-wearing people that we encountered at the museum, the free market, and the kindergarten. This is indeed an amazing coincidence, when you consider how big China reportedly is.

The Peking Duck is pretty good, but not plentiful, only a couple of small pieces per person. John informs us that in China, when you eat Peking Duck, you eat only the skin.

"Sure," mutters an Australian woman at our table. "And they'll tell the next group that you eat only the meat."

After lunch we're back on the bus, on the road to the major city of Guangzhou, which most Westerners know as Canton. John is pointing out that we are passing many shops, which is true, but the vast majority of them seem to be either (a) permanently under construction or (b) selling used tires.

In a few minutes we encounter dramatic proof that China's population is 1.1 billion: At *least* that many people are in a traffic jam with us. I have never seen a traffic jam like this—a huge, confused, gear-grinding, smoke-spewing, kaleidoscopic mass of vehicles, on the road and on the shoulders, stretching for miles and miles, every single driver simultaneously honking and attempting to change lanes. Our driver, Bill, puts on a wondrous show of skill, boldly bluffing other drivers, displaying lightning reflexes and great courage, aiming for spaces that I would not have attempted in a go-kart. Watching him, we passengers become swept up in the drama, our palms sweating each time he makes yet another daring, seemingly impossible move that will, if it succeeds, gain us maybe two whole feet.

We pass an exciting hour and a half this way, finally arriving at the source of the problem, which is, needless to say, a Repair Crew. Providing security are a half-dozen men who look like police officers or soldiers, standing around smoking and talking, ignoring the crazed traffic roiling past them. The work crew itself consists of eight men, seven of whom are watching one man, who's sitting in the middle of the highway holding a hammer and a chisel. As we inch past, this man is carefully positioning the chisel on a certain spot on the concrete. It takes him a minute or so to get it exactly where he wants it, then, with great care, he raises the hammer and strikes the chisel. I can just barely hear the *ping* over the sound of the honking. The man lifts the chisel up to evaluate the situation. I estimate that, barring unforeseen delays, this particular repair job should easily be completed in 12,000 years. These guys are *definitely* qualified to do highway repair in the U.S.

We are running late when we get to Canton, where we have a happy reunion with our fellow sticker-wearing, museum-going duck-skin-eaters from the other buses at the Canton Zoo. I don't want to sound like a broken record here, but this is a grim and seedy zoo, an Animal's

96

Republic of China, all cracked concrete and dirty cages. The other zoo-goers seem more interested in us tourists than in the animals, staring as we pass. We're shepherded to the pandas and the monkeys, then into a special, foreigners-only area to buy souvenirs. I buy my son a little green hat styled like the one Chairman Mao used to wear, with a red star on the front. Radical chic.

Back on the bus, we drive through Canton's streets, which are teeming with people on bicycles, forming major bicycle traffic jams. Imagine all the bicycles in the world, then double this amount, and you have an idea of Canton at rush hour. We pass a large market, where, John assures us, you can buy any kind of snake you want. Fortunately, we don't stop; we're going to see the Temple of the Six Banyans, which no longer has any banyans, although it does have three large brass statues of Buddha, which John claims are the largest brass Buddha statues in Guangzhou Province, and I don't doubt it for a minute. Next we head for the Dr. Sun Yat-Sen Memorial Hall, which is quite impressive and which boasts the largest brass statue of *any kind* in Guangzhou Province. Out front is a sign recounting the hall's history in English, including this mysterious sentence: "In 1988, the Guangzhou municipality had allocated funds for get rid of the hidden electrical danger in the hall Comprehensively."

Next we're scheduled to see the Statue of the Five Goats, but we're running out of time, which is a shame because I'm sure it's the largest statue of the five goats in Guangzhou Province. Instead we go to the Hotel of the Western-Style Toilets, the lobby of which is bustling with sticker-wearers rushing to get to the restrooms and back to the buses. There's only one more train back to Hong Kong tonight, and nobody wants to miss it.

We reach the train station in a heavy downpour. Led by

our Hong Kong guide, Tommy, we press our way through the crowds to the security checkpoint, then board Train No. 97 for Hong Kong. It's a fascinating train, a long way from the sterile, snack-bar ambience of Amtrak. Train No. 97 has funky old coaches with wide aisles, through which women push carts offering food, drinks, snacks, and duty-free cognac. The train also has a crowded, smoky dining car, a kitchen, people in uniform watching you, people who are not in uniform but are still watching you, and various little rooms and passages with people going in and out. It's a mysterious little world unto itself, Train No. 97. Walking through the rocking cars as night falls over the rice paddies outside, I feel like a character in a melo-drama. *The Last Train to Hong Kong.* Two of my fellow sticker-wearers walk past me, smiling, one of them wearing a souvenir Mao-style hat. This is *cool*, being on a train in Red China. As long as you can get out.

In three hours we're back in Hong Kong, which felt so foreign this morning but which now feels familiar and safe, like Des Moines. I rip my sticker off, a free man. I still don't know anything about China. I'm just one more su-perficial sheeplike bus-riding tourist. But I know this: I don't want to be in Hong Kong after June 30, 1997.

Tick tick tick tick tick . . .

As we're saying good-bye to Tommy, I ask him what he's going to do. He answers instantly.

"I'm going to marry a Westerner and get out of here," he says. He's laughing, but I'm not sure that he's kidding.

The next morning we read in the *Hongkong Standard* about two things that happened on the day we were in China:

- The chief of public security for the area we visited was executed. He'd been found guilty of corruption the previous day (none of those pesky appeals in the People's Republic). Among other things, he accepted bribes in exchange for letting people get out of China.

- In Beijing, the *People's Daily* ran a front-page editorial calling for a "great wall of iron" to protect China from "hostile forces," particularly democracy. The editorial said that if China's 1989 prodemocracy movement had succeeded, "it would have been a catastrophe for the people and a step back for history."

Those wild and crazy Chinese leaders! Those happy-go-lucky, fun-loving, Most-Favored-Nation guys! They're going to have a *ball* with Hong Kong. My advice is, see it while you can.

Tick tick tick tick tick . . .

And if anybody out there is in the market for a tall, likable English-speaking Chinese husband, I know of a guy who might be available.

HAUTE HOLES

You'll be pleased to learn that I have thought up yet another way to revive our nation's sagging economy by making myself rich.

To understand my concept, you need to be aware of an important fashion trend sweeping the entire nation (defined as "parts of New York and San Francisco"). Under this trend, sophisticated urban persons, seeking leisure wear, are purchasing used, beat-up, worn, ripped, raggedy cowboy garments that were previously owned by actual cowboys. People are actually paying *more* for damaged cowboy jeans than for new ones.

I found out about this trend through the alertness of reader Suzanne Hough, who sent me an article by Maria Recio of the *Fort Worth Star-Telegram*. The article states that used cowboy jeans are selling briskly at $50 a pair in San Francisco and $65 a pair in New York. The ones with holes are considered most desirable. Here are two quotes about this trend from the article:

FROM THE OWNER OF A NEW YORK CITY STORE THAT SELLS THE JEANS: "It gives a bit of romance."

FROM AN ACTUAL TEXAS COWBOY: "It sounds pretty stupid."

Of course it is exactly this shortsighted lack of fashion consciousness on the part of cowboys that keeps them stuck in dead-end jobs where they must become involved with actual cows. Meanwhile your fashion visionaries such as Mr. Ralph "Hombre" Lauren—people who truly understand the *spirit* of the West—have made so much money in recent years selling designer lines of Pretend Cowboy clothing that they can afford to build large tasteful pretend ranch estates with color-coordinated sagebrush.

But now we have gone, as a nation, beyond Pretend

le Jeanerie

WORN BY FAMOUS
BULL RIDER!
(THE LATE LARRY
"CHEEKS" O'MELVIN.)
$129.95

Cowboy fashions, and into Formerly Real Cowboy fashions. I called several stores, and they told me the demand for used jeans is very strong.

"People want holes in the knees, crotch, and buns," stated Murray Selkow, a Philadelphia native who now owns the Wild Wild West store in San Francisco. "What's very popular is two tears right at the bottom of the buns."

To locate the source of cowboy jeans I called Montana, a large cow-intensive state located near Canada. I spoke with Judy MacFarlane, who owns a company called Montana Broke, located outside a small town called (really) Manhattan. She buys used jeans from cowboys and sells them to stores such as Wild Wild West.

"I will not accept any jeans unless they're from a bona fide cattle rancher, rodeo rider, or sheriff's posseman," she told me. She said each pair of Montana Broke jeans comes with a label explaining the occupation of the cowboy who owned it, plus a "Tracking Guide," which shows the purchaser how to figure out which specific cowboy activities caused the various holes, stains, and worn spots on the jeans. I'm sure this provides hours of enjoyment for urban professionals, who, after a hard day of wrangling sales reports, can mosey back to their condominiums, rustle up a mess o' sushi, and spend an old-fashioned Western-style evening analyzing their jean damage. ("Oh, look, Jennifer! This brown mark on the knee occurred when the cowboy branded a calf! Or fell into a cow pie!" "Oh, Brad! That just makes me want to roll back the Oriental rug and initiate a hoedown!")

This trend is not limited to jeans. The store owners I talked to said there is also a strong demand for used cowboy jackets, shirts, boots, and hats. This leads me to my money-making idea, which is going to seem so obvious when I tell you that you're going to smack yourself in the forehead for not thinking of it first. My idea is to *sell used cowboy underwear by mail.* Don't laugh. This is the logical next step, and I'm going to be out front on it. My brand will be called: Buckaroo Briefs. Each brief will come with an authentic piece of old-looking paper with a diagram explaining how the briefs came to look the way they do ("This particular stain occurred when the cowboy got chased by a bull").

The only problem I see, looking ahead, is that with the increasing big-city demand for authentic Western garments of all kinds, and the relatively small number of actual rural Westerners, we're going to reach a point fairly soon where the entire population of Montana is running around naked. Fortunately, I've thought of a way to solve this problem via ANOTHER money-making concept, namely: *Sell urban professionals' used business attire to cowboys.* Why not? Cowboys in suits! Carrying their lassos in briefcases! It might catch on. You could probably even charge them more for the suits with really exciting histories ("This rip occurred when Thad, rushing to an important budget meeting, caught his sleeve on the fax machine").

Pretty sharp idea, huh? I don't see how it can miss. The only possible flaw is that cowboys are not nearly stupid enough to pay extra for somebody else's used and damaged clothing. I doubt that even the cows are.

COURTROOM
CONFESSIONS

—————

Like most people, I can always use an extra $7 or $8 million, which is why today I have decided to write a blockbuster legal thriller.

Americans buy legal thrillers by the ton. I was in many airports over the past few months, and I got the impression that aviation authorities were making this announcement over the public-address system: "FEDERAL REGULATIONS PROHIBIT YOU FROM BOARDING A PLANE UNLESS YOU ARE CARRYING *THE CLIENT* BY JOHN GRISHAM." I mean, *everybody* had this book. ("This is the captain speaking. We'll be landing in Seattle instead of Detroit because I want to finish *The Client*.")

The ironic thing is that best-selling legal thrillers generally are written by lawyers, who are not famous for written communication. I cite as Exhibit A my own attorney, Joseph DiGiacinto, who is constantly providing me with shrewd advice that I cannot understand because Joe has taken the legal precaution of translating it into Martian.

Usually, when people send you a fax, they send a cover page on top of it, which conveys the following information: "Here's a fax for (your name)." But Joe's cover page

features a statement approximately the length of the U.S. Constitution, worded so legally that I can't look directly at it without squinting. It says something like: ''WARNING: The following document and all appurtenances thereto and therein are the sole and exclusionary property of the aforementioned (hereinafter 'The Mortgagee') and may not be read, touched, spindled, fondled or rebroadcast without the expressively written consent of Major League Baseball, subject to severe legal penalties (hereinafter 'The Blowtorch Noogie') this means YOU.''

And that's just Joe's *cover page*. Nobody has ever dared to read one of his actual faxes, for fear of being immediately thrown into prison.

Nevertheless, some lawyers are hugely successful writers, and I intend to cash in on this. I am not, technically, a lawyer, but I did watch numerous episodes of "Perry Mason," and on one occasion, when I got a traffic ticket, I represented myself in court, successfully pleading *nolo contendere* (Latin, meaning "Can I pay by check?"). So I felt well qualified to write the following blockbuster legal thriller and possible movie screenplay:

CHAPTER ONE

The woman walked into my office, and I instantly recognized her as Clarissa Fromage, charged with murdering her late husband, wealthy industrial polluter A. Cranston "Bud" Fromage, whose death was originally reported as a heart attack but later ruled a homicide when sophisticated laboratory tests showed that his head had been cut off.

"So," she said. "You're a young Southern lawyer resembling a John Grisham protagonist as much as possible without violating the copyright."

"That's right," I replied. "Perhaps we can have sex."

"Not in the first chapter," she said.

CHAPTER TWO

"Ohhhhhhh," she cried out. "OOOHMIGOD."

"I'm sorry," I said, "but that's my standard hourly fee."

CHAPTER THREE

The courtroom tension was so palpable that you could feel it.

"Detective Dungman," said the district attorney, "please tell the jury what you found inside the defendant's purse on the night of the murder."

"Tic-Tacs," said Dungman.

"Was there anything else?"

"No, I can't think of . . . Wait a minute. Now that you mention it, there *was* something."

"What was it?"

"A chain saw."

A murmur ran through the courtroom and, before the bailiff could grab it, jumped up and bit Judge Webster M. Tuberhonker on the nose.

"That's going to hurt," I told my client.

CHAPTER FOUR

With time running out on the case, we returned to my office for a scene involving full frontal nudity.

CHAPTER FIVE

A hush fell over the courtroom, injuring six, as I approached the witness.

"Dr. Feldspar," I said. "You are an expert, are you not?"

"Yes," he answered.

"And you are familiar with the facts of this case, are you not?"

"Yes."

"And you are aware that, as a trained attorney, I can turn statements into questions by ending them with 'are you not,' are you not?"

"Yes."

"And is it not possible that, by obtaining genetic material from fossils, scientists could clone NEW dinosaurs?"

"OBJECTION!" thundered the district attorney. "He's introducing the plot from the blockbuster science thriller and motion picture *Jurassic Park!*"

The judge frowned at me over his spectacles. "In the movie," he said, "whom do you see playing the defendant in Chapter Four?"

"Sharon Stone," I answered.

"I'll allow it."

CHAPTER SIX

"And so, ladies and gentlemen of the jury," I said, "only ONE PERSON could have committed this murder, and that person is . . ."

The guilty party suddenly jumped up, causing the courtroom to nearly spit out its chewing gum.

"THAT'S RIGHT!" the guilty party shouted. "I DID IT, AND I'M GLAD!"

It was Amy Fisher.

READER ALERT

Except for the column about zebra mussels clinging to the giant brassiere, this next section is about boating. I own a motorboat, named *Buster*, who appears a couple of times in this section. In fact, Buster appears in this section considerably more often than he appears in the actual water. Buster spends most of his time sitting in my driveway. Every now and then I'll try to start him, thereby causing a couple of his key engine parts to fall off. Then I call the smiling mechanic, who tows Buster away, fixes him, and tows him back to my driveway, where he (Buster) sits for a couple of months, chuckling softly and slowly working his engine parts loose for the next time that I try to start him.

The sea: It's my life.

OVER HIS HEAD

Summer is here again, and as the official spokesperson for the recreational boating industry, I've been asked to remind you that boating is a fun and relaxing family activity with very little likelihood that your boat will sink and you'll wind up bobbing helplessly in the water while sharks chew on your legs as if they were a pair of giant Slim Jims, *provided that you follow proper nautical procedures.*

Fortunately, I can tell you what these procedures are, because I am a veteran "salt" and the owner of a small motorboat, named *Buster Boat.* I spend many happy hours at Buster's helm, and I always feel totally safe, because I know that (a) most nautical dangers can be avoided through careful preparation, good seamanship, and common sense; and (b) Buster is sitting on a trailer in my yard. The biggest danger there is spiders, which like to make webs on Buster's seats because they've figured out that, statistically, Buster is less likely to wind up in the water than our house is.

Sometimes, when I'm sitting at the helm, killing spiders with the anchor, scanning the horizon of my yard for potential boating hazards, I turn on Buster's radio and listen to the Marine Forecast, which is always saying things like: "Barometer leaning to the southwest at 15 to 37 knots." As a recreational boater, you should be familiar with these nautical terms. For example, a "knot" means "about a mile an hour." There is a sound nautical reason why they don't come right out and *say* "about a mile an hour," namely, they want you, the recreational boater, to feel stupid. They used to be less subtle about it: In the old days, the Marine Forecast consisted entirely of a guy telling recreational-boater jokes. ("How many recreational boaters does it take to screw in a light bulb?" "They can't! Sharks have chewed off their arms!")

The Marine Forecast is always telling you obvious things,

such as which way the wind is blowing, which you can figure out for yourself just by watching the motion of your spiderwebs. They never tell you about the serious boating hazards, which are located—write down this Boating Safety Tip—*under the water*. It turns out that although the water is basically flat on top, underneath there are large hostile objects such as reefs and shoals (or "forecastles") that have been carelessly strewn around, often smack-dab in the path of recreational boaters.

I discovered this shocking fact recently when some friends visited us in Miami, and in a foolish effort to trick them into thinking that we sometimes go out on our boat, we actually went out on our boat. It was a good day for boating, with the barometer gusting at about 47 liters of mercury, and we had no problems until I decided to make the boat go forward. For some reason, motorboats are designed to go at only two speeds: "Virtually Stopped" and "Airborne." We were traveling along at Virtually Stopped, which seemed inadequate—barnacles were passing us—so I inched the throttle forward just a teensy bit and *WHOOOOMM* suddenly we were passengers on the Space Shuttle Buster. Every few feet Buster would launch himself completely out of the water and attain such an altitude that at any moment you expected flight attendants to appear with the beverage cart, and then *WHAM* Buster would crash down onto a particularly hard patch of water, causing our food and possessions and spiders to bounce overboard, forming a convenient trail for the sharks to follow. ("Look!" the sharks were saying. "A set of dentures! It won't be long now!")

In this relaxing and recreational manner we lurched toward downtown Miami, with me shouting out the various Points of Interest. "I THINK THAT'S A DRUG DEAL-ER!" I would shout. Or: "THERE GOES ANOTHER

POSSIBLE DRUG DEALER!'' I was gesturing toward these long, sleek motorboats with about 14 engines apiece that you see roaring around the Miami waters driven by men with no apparent occupation other than polishing their neck jewelry.

So it was a pleasant tropical scene, with the wind blowing and the sea foaming and the sun glinting off the narcotics traffickers. As the captain, I was feeling that pleasant sense of well-being that comes from being in total command and not realizing that you are heading directly toward a large underwater pile of sand. I would say we hit it at about 630 knots, so that when Buster skidded to a cartoon-style stop, we were in about six inches of water, a depth that the U.S. Coast Guard recommends for craft classified as ''Popsicle sticks or smaller.'' This meant that, to push Buster off the sand, my friend John and I had to go *into the water,* which lapped threateningly around our lower shins. Probably the only thing that saved our lives was that the dreaded Man-Eating But Really Flat Shark was not around.

So we did survive, and I'm already looking forward to our next recreational boating outing, possibly as soon as the next century. Perhaps, if you're a boater, you'll see me out there! I'll be the one wearing shin guards.

MOBY DAVE

In Which a Mysterious Sea Captain's Obsession with the Great White Bonefish Leads His Faithful Vessel and Crew Directly into the Bizarre Vortex of the Lethargy Zone. And a Lot of Beer

You can't explain it, this need that men have to go to sea. I sure can't explain it. One day it just seized me, like a case of the hives.

"Beth," I said to my wife. "Let's take Buster to Bimini."

Buster is our boat. It usually sits on a trailer in our backyard, forming an ideal natural habitat for spiders. Spiders come from as far away as Brazil to make their homes on Buster.

Bimini is a place out in the Atlantic Ocean. The main thing I knew about Bimini was that it was where Gary Hart went to establish himself as a leading former presidential contender. I wasn't even 100 percent sure what country, legally, Bimini belonged to. But I did know that people regularly went there from Miami in their boats. When I announced that I was going to Bimini, many people felt compelled to tell me confidence-building anecdotes about their trips.

"Oh, yeah," they'd say. "One time I was halfway there, and this storm came up and the wind was 83 miles an hour and there were 27-foot waves and the engine conked out and the radio broke and we all got sick and my wife suddenly went into labor even though she *wasn't even pregnant* and a huge tentacle came out of the water and snatched Ashley and . . .''

The reason this kind of thing can happen is that, even though Bimini is only about 50 miles from Miami, to get to it you have to go right through the famous Bermuda Triangle, which is formed by drawing lines between Bermuda, the Bahamas, and my driveway. Terrible things happen constantly in this area, with I-95 being only one example. Also, flowing right through the Bermuda Triangle, between Miami and Bimini, is the famous Gulf Stream, which serves as a giant, natural rapid mass-transit system for sharks.

So I knew that, before I attempted to cross to Bimini, I had to get Buster Boat into shape. Step one was to take him to a mechanic, because several things had gone wrong with him while he'd been sitting on his trailer. This is normal. A major law of physics is that things decay faster on a boat than in any other environment. Scientists have attempted to measure this phenomenon, but their instruments keep breaking. If a screw falls off your boat, and you go to a marine-supply store to buy a replacement—which will cost you several times as much as an ordinary civilian screw, because of course it has to be a *marine* screw—you can sometimes see your new screw actually dissolving on the counter *while you're still paying for it.*

So I took Buster to the mechanic, Dan, and he got everything working, and while I was writing the check I mentioned that I was going to Bimini.

Dan gave me a concerned look.

"You're going to *Bimini?*" he asked.

"Yes," I said, over the sound of Buster decaying in the background.

"You better get some spare parts," he said. He started naming things like "transgressor nodule" and "three-sixteenths retribution valve." I wrote it all down, went to the marine-supply store, and dutifully purchased every item on the list, although it would have been simpler to just pick up the Big Economy Box O' Random Parts, because my mechanical skills are limited to annually installing the new registration decal on my car license plate. If Buster conked out in the Gulf Stream, I would sit in the exact center of the boat and throw engine parts at the sharks.

But I was as ready as I was going to get. So early one Friday morning in July, Beth and I arose and—as bold seafaring people have done for thousands of years—went to a bakery. "Never attempt to cross the Gulf Stream without fresh pastries" is one of the Coast Guard's Rules for Safe Boating. Then we drove to where we'd put Buster into the water earlier, climbed aboard, and headed out to sea, with fear in our hearts and crumbs in our laps.

At this point I need to get technical for a moment and explain how to navigate to Bimini. Bimini is roughly east of Miami, so the simplest approach would be to steer a compass course of approximately 90 degrees Fahrenheit longitude. However, you also have to consider the fact that the Gulf Stream flows northward at an average of 2.5 amps, although this varies in certain areas depending on local shark motion. And then there are your winds, your tides, your barometric pressure, your jellyfish, your big, disgusting wads of floating seaweed, and your solar eclipses, one of which had occurred the day before we left. Taking all of these factors into consideration, I examined the charts, did a few navigational calculations, and decided that the best way to get to Bimini would be to follow Steele's boat.

Steele is Howard Steele Reeder II, a friend of ours who had graciously agreed to lead us to Bimini. He's a boating enthusiast, although that phrase seems too weak to describe the level of his interest, kind of like describing someone as a "heroin fancier." Steele, like most boating enthusiasts, is always in the process of simultaneously (a) fixing something on his current boat and (b) thinking about trading it in for another boat with a new and different set of decaying parts. For the Bimini voyage, he had to borrow his brother's boat, because his own boat, which he had just bought, had already broken. Soon the marine industry will develop a boat that is prebroken right at the factory. When they finish building it, they'll just tow it out into the middle of the Gulf Stream and sink it, then hand you the bill of sale. Boating enthusiasts will be in heaven.

On board with Steele were his wife, Bobette, and another couple, Linda and Olin McKenzie. Olin is a dentist. "Never attempt to cross the Gulf Stream without a qualified dentist" is another one of the Coast Guard's Rules for Safe Boating. Too many maritime tragedies could easily have been avoided if the victims had been more aware of the insidious dangers of plaque formation.

But the most important passenger on Steele's boat was the Loran unit. This is a little electronic device that somehow, we think by magic, *knows where Bimini is.* "It's over there!" says the Loran, via little electronic arrows. This is a truly wonderful navigational aid, and I hope that someday it will be installed in every automobile, because it would be pretty funny to see thousands of cars driving, at 55 miles per hour, into the Atlantic Ocean.

So Steele followed the Loran, and we followed Steele, bouncing along in Buster. Buster is not one of those big, heavy, Orson Welles–style boats that plow sedately through the sea. Buster is a small, light, Richard Simmons–style boat that likes to skip gaily across the tops of the waves, churning your internal organs into pudding.

So we bounced through Biscayne Bay and out into the Atlantic. The tall buildings of downtown Miami grew smaller and smaller behind us (actually, they stayed the same size; they only *appeared* to get smaller, because of the Greenhouse Effect). There was nothing in front of us except water, which was dark blue, because the Gulf Stream is approximately 23.6 million feet deep. Anything could be lurking down there. There could be things down there with eyeballs the size of your entire boat. It's best not to think about it. It's best not to look ahead, either, because there's an alarming quantity of nothing out there. It's best to look wistfully back at Miami, getting smaller and smaller and smaller. At times, in the past, I had been critical of Miami, but out there at sea I was becoming a major civic booster. I was realizing that Miami has a lot of excellent qualities, the main one being that it is not located in the Gulf Stream. If your engine breaks down in Miami, all you have to do is pull your car over to the side of the road, put the hood up, and wait for a passing motorist to take a shot at you. But that seemed safer than being out in the ocean, relying entirely on two smallish boats and a little electronic device. What if the Loran wasn't pointing us to Bimini at all? What if Steele's brother forgot to pay his Loran bill, and the device, chuckling electronically to itself, was steering us to Iceland?

These thoughts ran through my mind as I munched pensively on a poppy-seed muffin and Miami got smaller, and smaller, and smaller, and finally . . .

Miami was *gone*. There was nothing behind us, nothing ahead of us, nothing on either side, except water. I didn't look down because I didn't want to catch even a *glimpse* of a giant eyeball. I kept my eyes Krazy Glued to the back of

Steele's boat, trusting that he would . . . HEY! What the HELL is Steele doing? He's STOPPING! Out HERE!!

"WHAT IS IT?" I shouted.

"FISH!" Steele said.

That's right: There we were, in extremely deep water, completely out of sight of civilization, probably miles off course, possibly with icebergs drifting our way, and Steele and Olin had decided to try to catch *fish*, which are readily available in cooked form at any decent restaurant. So for the longest 10 minutes of my life, Steele and Olin fished while I circled them. I didn't dare stop Buster, for fear that he'd decide the trip was over and refuse to go again.

Finally, thank God, Olin caught a fish, which he released because it was too small. Your true sportsperson prefers a fish that is large enough so that when you cut it open, it spews slime all over the entire boat. But the fish had satisfied Olin's and Steele's urge to angle, and soon we were off again.

We bounced along for another hour, with nothing appearing on the horizon. At one point, Steele and Olin went through an elaborate pantomime for my benefit: They got out a chart, looked at it, shrugged elaborately, pointed in opposite directions, and had a big arm-waving argument. This was of course highly entertaining to me. "What a pair of wacky cutups!" I said to myself. "If we ever reach land, I will kill them with my emergency signal flare gun!"

Finally, after 2½ hours, which in a small, bouncing boat feels approximately as long as the Reagan administration, Steele pointed to the horizon ahead. I looked out, and experiencing the same emotion that Columbus must have felt when he first caught sight of the Statue of Liberty, I saw: nothing. But a few minutes later I thought I saw something dark and low against the sky, so I strained my eyeballs and ... Yes! There it was! Bimini! Or possibly Iceland! I didn't care. At least we were *somewhere*.

"Good *boy*, Buster," I said, patting him on his compass. Praise is crucial to proper boat maintenance.

A half hour later we reached Bimini harbor, arriving at the same time as a Chalk's seaplane, which got there from Miami in about 25 minutes (this is known, among us nautical sea salts, as the Wussy Method). The harbor was full of huge recreational boats that cost millions of dollars and burn hundreds of gallons of fuel per afternoon so that sportspersons, equipped with thousands of dollars worth of tackle and tens of thousands of dollars worth of electronic equipment, can locate and sometimes even catch fish worth up to $3.59 per pound.

A lot of people go to Bimini to find fish, especially the wily bonefish. There are many local guides who will take you out looking for bonefish; they're all nicknamed "Bonefish," as in Bonefish Willie, Bonefish Sam, Bonefish Irving, Bonefish e. e. cummings, etc. While in Bimini I tried hard to get my traveling companions to refer to me as "Bonefish Dave," but it never caught on.

It turns out that Bimini is part of the Bahamas, which is, technically, a completely different country. This meant that we had to go through Immigration and Customs. I have never understood the point of this process. I assume they want to make sure you're not bringing in bales of cocaine, or an undesirable person such as Charles Manson, or some agricultural threat such as the Deadly Bonefish Rot. But in most places they hardly even look at you. In Bimini they didn't even look at our boats. Instead they handed us a bunch of forms, which we spent about an hour and a half filling out and getting stamped by various uniformed officials. (They're big on stamping things; I imagine that about once a week a big ink tanker steams into the harbor to replenish the supply.)

If *I* designed Customs forms, they'd have questions like:

1. Are you bringing in any cocaine?
2. How about Charles Manson?

And so on. But the Bahamas' forms didn't ask anything like this. Instead, they asked—this is a real question—"Has plague occurred or been suspected among rats or mice on board during the voyage, or has there been unusual mortality among them?" How are you supposed to answer a question like that? Go down into the bowels of the boat, locate a spokesrat or spokesmouse, and say, "Any unusual mortality around here?" So I answered: No. I figured that if Buster contained any kind of animal life, it would be spiders, and they would be too severely vibrated to cause any problems.

The worst part of the Bimini Customs and Immigration procedure was that periodically one of the officials would ask me, in front of other boaters, the name of my boat (or, as they put it, my "vessel"). The other boaters all had bold masculine boat names like *Sea Biceps* and *Testosterone Torpedo*, so I felt inadequate:

CUSTOMS OFFICIAL: What is the name of the vessel?

ME (quietly): *Buster Boat.*

CUSTOMS OFFICIAL (loudly): *Buster Boat?*

ME (very quietly): Yes.

CUSTOMS OFFICIAL: And you are the master of the vessel?

ME: Well, I was *steering* it, yes, but I was basically following Steele, because . . .

CUSTOMS OFFICIAL: What is the name of the vessel again?

Finally they decided that we were not a serious threat to the Bahamian national security, so they let us in. And I'm glad they did, because Bimini is wonderful. The most wonderful thing about it is that, because of the prevailing winds, currents, tides, rum supply, etc., Bimini is located smack-dab in the center of what scientists believe to be the world's most powerful Lethargy Zone. It is extremely difficult to remain tense there. The moment you arrive, lethargy waves start washing over you, seeping into your body, turning your skeletal system into taffy. You stop worrying about things like your job, your mortgage, your kids, whether the recession will last, whether your fly is unzipped, etc. You function on a more basic level, concerning yourself with issues such as: Should I scratch my armpit now? Or later? If you stand in one place too long, you can become so relaxed that you sink to the ground and form a very carefree puddle.

"See that puddle over there?" people will say, pointing to a blob of flesh on the dock. "That used to be the chairman of the Federal Reserve Board. He was supposed to stop in Bimini for just a couple of hours—this was in 1958—but the lethargy got to him before he even got off the dock. We think there's still a pair of wing-tipped shoes under there somewhere. Twice a day we pour a pitcher of daiquiris on him, and he's happy."

If you want objective proof of the Lethargy Zone's effects, take a look at the famous photograph of Gary Hart in Bimini, sitting against a dock piling with Donna Rice on his lap. Notice how relaxed his body is. Notice the goofy smile on his face. Here's a guy thinking, "OK, on the one hand, I have a serious shot at becoming president of the United States, leader of the Free World, the most powerful person on the face of the Earth; on the other hand, I can sit here with a hot babe on my lap." On Bimini, this is an easy choice.

Geographically, Bimini is divided into two major parts:

1. The water.
2. The land.

The water is clear and warm and blue and beautiful. It contains numerous scenic fish as well as some highly relaxed conchs and the occasional airplane that crashed while attempting to bring in illegal narcotics at night back in the Bad Old '80s, before the government cracked down, when smuggling was a major local industry. (I wonder what those pilots put on *their* Customs questionnaires? Maybe: "There was unusual mortality among the mice and rats caused by the plane hitting the water at 120 mph.")

But the land is my favorite part. It's really just a few little islands, altogether less than 10 square miles, with about 1,500 residents, 75 liquor licenses, and a group of friendly, casual, closely related dogs. Most of the development is on North Bimini, along a strip of land narrow enough that you could probably throw a rock from one side to the other, if you weren't feeling so lethargic. At the south end of the island is Bimini's metropolitan hub, Alice Town, which consists of a few dozen stores, T-shirt stands, restaurants, and flat-out bars. Most of the buildings' front doors open right onto the narrow street, which has no sidewalk, so that when you step outside, you're basically standing in the middle of the main island road. "Never step out of a bar in Bimini without carefully looking both ways, especially if you have been drinking the legendary Bahama Mama rum drink," is one of the Coast Guard's Rules for Walking Around Bimini.

Fortunately, there's not much traffic, and the drivers, many of them on motor scooters, cheerfully weave and beep their way through the pedestrians, usually missing everybody, which is a lot more than you can say for drivers in Miami. People in Bimini are friendly. This is a generalization, but it's true, anyway. People tend to say hi to you even if you're a flagrant tourist.

The Bimini stores give new meaning to the term "small business." Some of them could easily fit into a dressing room at Bloomingdale's. The window displays are eclectic—Bimini mugs, T-shirts, conch shells, a roll of film manufactured during the Carter administration—generally covered with a nice, relaxed layer of dust. A number of buildings are boarded up or missing key architectural elements such as a roof. Men were working inside one bright blue building called The Chic Store ("Bimini's Oldest, Established 1935"). A hand-lettered sign in the window said: SORRY FOR ANY INCONVENIENCE. CLOSED FOR RENERVATIONS.

The Chic Store was just down the street from Melvin's Fashion Center, which featured a nice selection of T-shirts, and Priscilla's Epicurean Delights ("To Thrill the Gourmet Palate"), which featured conch. Conch is one of Bimini's major palate thrills, served in fritters and salads, or as a main course. It's delicious, especially if you don't think about what it looked like before they cooked it. "Never think about the fact that a conch is basically a large underwater snail" is one of the Coast Guard's Rules for Eating Conch. Bimini also has a locally baked bread, sweet and heavy and highly addictive.

My favorite spot in downtown Bimini is an arch erected on the side of the road. It says:

BIMINI—GATEWAY TO
THE BAHAMAS
THE YOUTH DEPARTMENT
THE ORDER OF ELKS OF THE
WORLD (I.B.P.O.E. OF W.)
WELCOMES THE TOURIST
TO BIMINI

Underneath the arch is a little shrinelike display, featuring an arrangement of conch shells surrounding a toy rake, shovel, and hoe, pointing aloft. Next to this display is a small, mysterious sign that says:

TO BE AWARDED TROPHY
FOR BEST KEPT YARD.

To one side is a rusting antique hand fire-fighting pump. (Why not?)

Across the street is a sign that says:

GLENDA'S SCOOTER RENTAL
AND
THE FOUNTAIN OF YOUTH

Yes. Not only does Bimini have scooter rentals, but the Fountain of Youth is located there, over on South Bimini, according to legend. You can take tours to it. We didn't bother, because of being in the Lethargy Zone. We figured, hey, if we got young again, we'd have to go through young adulthood again—zits, career-building, etc.—and it just sounded so tiring that we decided to skip eternal youth and have some beers and conch fritters instead. We did this at one of Bimini's most famous social spots, the Compleat Angler hotel and bar, which is where famed novelist and macho hombre Ernest Hemingway used to hang out. One room is a sort of museum, with pictures of Hemingway all over the walls, including one with the following caption: "ERNEST HEMINGWAY SHOOTING THOMPSON MACHINE GUN, BIMINI DOCK." He liked to shoot guns at sharks. One time he got so excited, shooting at a shark, that—this is true—he shot himself in *both legs*. That's the kind of sportsperson Ernest was.

I have not begun to describe all the things you can see and do just in metropolitan Bimini. I have not mentioned the plaque commemorating the late congressperson Adam Clayton Powell, who spent a great deal of time in Bimini, drinking scotch and milk and no doubt thinking up ways to better represent his New York City constituents; or the Chalk's Seaplane Terminal with the antenna that looks like a Science Fair project made from coat hangers, where you can watch the plane come in and taxi right across the main road to discharge its passengers; or the End of the World Bar, whose floor is sand and whose walls seem to be made entirely of graffiti; or the Bimini bus, a van equipped with numerous bumper stickers and what appears to be a radar antenna. What with all the things to see, plus the lethargy factor, plus the beer, it took us a little over four hours to walk through Alice Town and back, a distance of several hundred yards. Of course, on the way back we were fighting a strong tide of passengers who had been released from the SeaEscape cruise ship for the afternoon and were sweeping down the island, snorking up rum and T-shirts.

Bimini attracts *all kinds* of people. One morning we watched as three men pulled up to a dock in a loooooooong motorboat, the kind shaped like a floating marital aid with numerous large engines on the back. They picked up a young woman wearing a practical nautical outfit consisting of an extremely tight, extremely short dress and spike-heeled shoes. She could barely move. She couldn't climb into the boat without causing her undergarments to be visible from Fort Lauderdale, so one of the men had to lift her into the boat like a large, high-heel-wearing sausage. Then off they roared, out to sea. Probably planning to do some snorkeling.

Bimini offers a wide range of nightlife activities. You can eat. You can drink. You can walk around the docks and watch sportspersons on large expensive boats slice fish apart and get slime and flies all over themselves and seem genuinely happy. You can eat some more. You can, if you are very fortunate, see Steele Reeder do his impression of how a conch looks at you when you have removed it from its shell ("*NOW* what??" the conch says). You can drink some more. You can dance, with or without a partner, in a bar or right on the street.

On Saturday night Olin and I were sitting at an outdoor bar, listening to a band called Glenn Rolle and the Surgeons. Three young women were dancing with each other. A man came dancing in off the street, nattily attired in shorts and an artificial leg. He danced up and joined the women, smiling blissfully. The four of them danced for a minute, then the man danced off, waving his artificial leg around in a manner that can only be described as joyful.

"There's a short story in there somewhere," remarked Olin.

I was so impressed by Glenn Rolle and the Surgeons that I went up to Rolle and asked if they had any record albums, and he sold me one for $5. When I got back to my table, I sensed that the album might be defective, inasmuch as it had a big bend in the middle, so you could easily fold it in half. Rolle cheerfully exchanged it for a new one, which I played when I got home. The album is called *Steal Away*. Side One consists of one song, called "Steal Away," which is a little over six minutes long. Side Two is also "Steal Away," but it's the instrumental version, which is identical to Side One but without the vocals. All in all, I think *Steal Away* is an excellent name for this album.

We honestly had planned to do more than just eat and drink and swim and laze on the beach and buy straw hats and walk around very slowly while burping during our stay in Bimini. We honestly intended to do some serious research on local points of interest, such as the Mysterious Underwater Thing Possibly Built by Aliens from Space. I am not making this point of interest up. It's called the

Bimini Road, and it consists of hundreds of big, flat rocks forming a half-mile-long, fairly regular pattern, shaped like a backward *J*, in 18 feet of water a half mile from Bimini. It was discovered in 1968, and many respected loons think that it has something to do with the Lost Continent of Atlantis. Others think it must have been aliens from space. It's a big mystery. How did it get there? What is it for?

My theory is that the space aliens were going to write a giant underwater backward message of advice for humanity starting with *J*, possibly "JUST DO IT." But after a short while in the Lethargy Zone they decided to knock off, maybe have a Bahama Mama, and before they knew it a couple of million years had passed and they had to return to their planet, leaving the message unfinished. Closed for renervations.

We were in a similar situation. Before we knew it, it was Sunday, time to head back to Miami, assuming that Miami still existed. There was no way to know for sure, because the Bimini phone system had been out of order the whole time we were there. I'm not sure telephones would have been all that effective, anyway. The speed of electricity on Bimini is probably around 10 miles per hour.

Anyway, we had children and jobs to get back to, and we were getting dangerously close to forming permanent flesh puddles. So after a well-balanced breakfast of about 17,000 pieces of Bimini-bread toast, we set out for home, with me, Master of the Vessel *Buster,* once again following Bonefish Howard Steele Reeder II, who was once again following the Loran.

In a couple of hours, Miami was on the horizon again, apparently intact, but I didn't dare to relax, because I knew that ahead of us lay the greatest maritime challenge of all, a hazard so dangerous that no sane boatperson would dream of attempting it: Biscayne Bay on a Sunday afternoon. You know how sometimes you're driving on I-95 in heavy traffic, and some substance abuser driving a car whose windows are tinted with what appears to be roofing tar weaves past you at 127 miles per hour, using all available lanes *plus* the median strip, and you say to yourself: "Why don't they get that lunatic OFF THE ROAD??" Well, trust me, on Sunday afternoon he *is* off the road. He and all his friends from the South Florida Maniac Drivers Club are all out on Biscayne Bay, roaring around in severely overpowered boats, looking for manatees to turn into Meatloaf of the Sea.

But we made it through without getting killed, which was too bad because it meant we had to go through the U.S. Customs procedure, which is even sillier than the Bahamian one. It was developed by the hardworking Federal Bureau of Irritating Procedures That May Seem Pointless But Actually Accomplish Nothing. The way it works is, you have to report in from a special U.S. Customs telephone. The phone we went to is right next to a dock at the Crandon Park marina. But you can't *stop* at the dock unless you're buying fuel there. So the boat pulls up, and the captain gets off, and the boat has to leave—ideally with somebody driving it—and drift around the marina with all the other incoming motorboats, sailboats, Cuban refugee rafters, etc., while the captain gets in line to wait for the phone. It can take an hour or more for your turn, and when you finally get to talk to the Customs people, they want to know things like your Social Security number and birth date. How this information helps them protect the borders is beyond me. I suppose that if you have something really important to tell them, such as that you're carrying illegal aliens or a bale of hashish, it's your responsibility to blurt this information out. Then I imagine you're supposed to put handcuffs on yourself, take a taxi to a federal prison, ring the bell, and wait until they find time to let you in.

Eventually, they decided that our Social Security numbers had enough digits, or whatever criterion they use, and they let us back into the United States, and we went home. But we've already decided we're going back to Bimini. I think *everybody* should go to Bimini from time to time. I think President Bush and whoever is governing the Soviet Union this afternoon should meet there. They would definitely have a more relaxed kind of summit.

ALICE TOWN, BAHAMAS—In a surprise development, the leaders of the two superpowers announced today that they have learned all the words, in English AND Russian, to "Conch Ain't Got No Bone."

Maybe you should go to Bimini, too. Maybe I'll even see you there, and we can wave to each other, if we're not feeling too lethargic.

Please address me as "Bonefish Dave."

SHARK BAIT

It began as a fun nautical outing, 10 of us in a motorboat off the coast of Miami. The weather was sunny and we saw no signs of danger, other than the risk of sliding overboard because every exposed surface on the boat was covered with a layer of snack-related grease. We had enough cholesterol on board to put the entire U.S. Olympic team into cardiac arrest. This is because all 10 of us were guys.

I hate to engage in gender stereotyping, but when women plan the menu for a recreational outing, they usually come up with a nutritionally balanced menu featuring all the major food groups, including the Sliced Carrots Group, the Pieces of Fruit Cut into Cubes Group, the Utensils Group, and the Plate Group. Whereas guys tend to focus on the Carbonated Malt Beverages Group and the Fatal Snacks Group. On this particular trip, our food supply consisted of about 14 bags of potato chips and one fast-food fried-chicken Giant Economy Tub o' Fat. Nobody brought, for example, napkins, the theory being that you could just wipe your hands on your stomach. Then you could burp. This is what guys on all-guy boats are

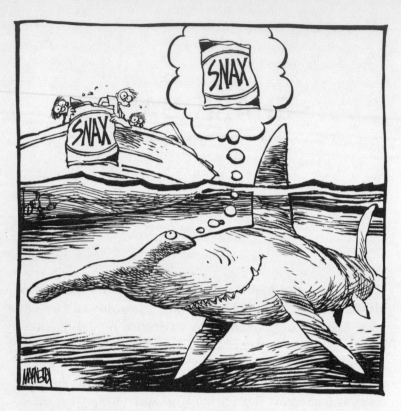

doing while women are thinking about their relationships.

The reason the grease got smeared everywhere was that four of the guys on the boat were 10-year-olds, who, because of the way their still-developing digestive systems work, cannot chew without punching. This results in a lot of dropped and thrown food. On this boat, you regularly encountered semignawed pieces of chicken skittering across the deck toward you like small but hostile alien creatures from the Kentucky Fried Planet. Periodically a man would yell "CUT THAT OUT!" at the boys, then burp to indicate the depth of his concern. Discipline is vital on a boat.

We motored through random-looking ocean until we

found exactly what we were looking for: a patch of random-looking ocean. There we dropped anchor and dove for Florida lobsters, which protect themselves by using their tails to scoot backward really fast. They've been fooling predators with this move for millions of years, but the guys on our boat, being advanced life forms, including a dentist, figured it out in under three hours.

I myself did not participate, because I believe that lobsters are the result of a terrible genetic accident involving nuclear radiation and cockroaches. I mostly sat around, watching guys lunge out of the water, heave lobsters into the boat, burp, and plunge back in. Meanwhile, the lobsters were scrabbling around in the chicken grease, frantically trying to shoot backward through the forest of legs belonging to 10-year-old boys squirting each other with gobs of the No. 197,000,000,000 Sun Block that their moms had sent along. It was a total Guy Day, very relaxing, until the arrival of the barracuda.

This occurred just after we'd all gotten out of the water. One of the men, Larry, was fishing, and he hooked a barracuda right where we had been swimming. This was unsettling. The books all say that barracuda rarely eat people, but very few barracuda can read, and they have *far* more teeth than would be necessary for a strictly seafood diet. Their mouths look like the entire $39.95 set of Ginsu knives, including the handy Arm Slicer.

We gathered around to watch Larry fight the barracuda. His plan was to catch it, weigh it, and release it with a warning. After 10 minutes he almost had it to the boat, and we were all pretty excited for him, when all of a sudden . . .

Ba-DUMP . . . Ba-DUMP . . .

Those of you who you read music recognize this as the soundtrack from the motion picture *Jaws*. Sure enough, cruising right behind Larry's barracuda, thinking sushi, was: a shark. And not just *any* shark. It was a hammerhead shark, perennial winner of the coveted Oscar for Ugliest Fish. It has a weird, T-shaped head with a big eyeball on each tip, so that it can see around both sides of a telephone pole. This ability is of course useless for a fish, but nobody would dare try to explain this to a hammerhead.

The hammerhead, its fin breaking the surface, zigzagged closer to Larry's barracuda, then surged forward.

"Oh ****!" went Larry, reeling furiously.

CHOMP went the hammerhead, and suddenly Larry's barracuda was in a new weight division.

CHOMP went the hammerhead again, and now Larry was competing in an entirely new category, Fish Consisting of Only a Head.

The boys were staring at the remainder of the barracuda, deeply impressed.

"This is your leg," said the dentist. "This is your leg in *Jaws*. Any questions?"

The boys, for the first time all day, were quiet.

CAPTAINS
UNCOURAGEOUS

There comes a time in a man's life when he hears the call of the sea.

"Hey, YOU!" are the sea's exact words.

If the man has a brain in his head, he will hang up the phone immediately. That's what I should have done recently when I was called to sea by my friends Hannah and Paddy, who had rented a sailboat in the Florida Keys. They love to sail. Their dream is to quit their jobs and sail around the world, living a life of carefree adventure until their boat is sunk by an irate whale and they wind up drifting in a tiny raft and fighting over who gets to eat the sun block. At least that's the way I see it turning out.

The only safe way to venture onto the ocean is aboard a cruise ship the size of a rural school district. Even then you're not safe, because you might become trapped in your cabin due to bodily expansion. Cruise ships carry thousands of tons of high-calorie food, and under maritime law they cannot return to port until all of it has been converted into passenger fat. So there are at least eight feedings a day. Crew members often creep into cabins at night and use high-pressure hoses to shoot cheesecake directly down the throats of sleeping passengers.

But on cruise ships you rarely find yourself dangling from poles, which is more than I can say for the sailboat rented by Hannah and Paddy. The captain was a man named Dan, who used to be a race-car driver until he had heart trouble and switched from fast cars to sailboats, which are the slowest form of transportation on Earth with the possible exception of airline flights that go through O'Hare. Sometimes I suspect that sailboats never move at all, and the only reason they appear to go from place to place is continental drift.

Nevertheless, we were having a pleasant day on Captain

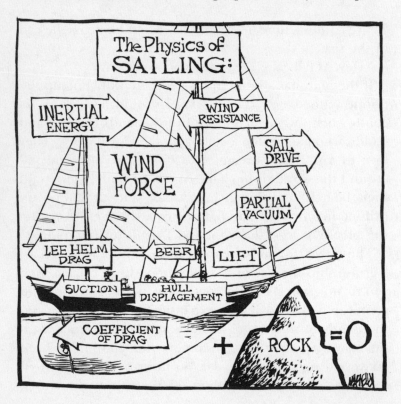

Dan's boat, the *Jersey Girl,* doing busy nautical things like hoisting the main stizzen and mizzening the aft beam, and meanwhile getting passed by other boats, seaweed, lobsters, glaciers, etc. The trouble arose when we attempted to enter a little harbor so we could go to a bar featuring a band headed by a large man named Richard. This band is called—really—Big Dick and the Extenders. We were close enough to hear them playing when the *Jersey Girl* plowed into what nautical experts call the "bottom."

The problem was an unusually low tide. Helpful people in smaller boats kept telling us this.

"It's an unusually low tide!" they'd shout helpfully as they went past. They were lucky the *Jersey Girl* doesn't have a cannon.

We'd been sitting there for quite a while when Captain Dan suggested, with a straight face, that if some of us held on to a large pole called the boom and swung out over the water, our weight might make the boat lean over enough to get free. I now realize that this was a prank. Fun-loving sailboat captains are probably always trying to get people out on the boom, but most people aren't that stupid.

We, however, had been substantially refreshed by beverages under a hot sun, so we actually did it. Four of us climbed up, hung our stomachs over the boom, kicked off from the side of the boat, and NOOOOOO . . .

Picture a giant shish-kebab skewer sticking out sideways from a boat 10 feet over the water, except instead of pieces of meat on it, there are four out-of-shape guys, faces pale and sweating, flabby legs flailing, ligaments snapping like rifle shots. We instantly became a tourist attraction. A crowd gathered on shore, laughing and pointing. Some of them were probably sailboat captains.

"Look!" they were probably saying. "Captain Dan got FOUR of them out on the boom! A new record!"

Meanwhile, next to me, Paddy, a middle-aged attorney who is not, let's be honest, built like an Olympic gymnast, who is in fact built a lot like a gym, was saying, in an unusually high voice, "We better bring the boom back now. OK? Now? OK?? WE BETTER BRING THE BOOM BACK NOW! BRINGTHEBOOMBACKNOW!! I SAID . . ."

"HANG ON!" Captain Dan was shouting. "She's about to move!"

People on shore were now taking pictures.

"IT'S AN UNUSUALLY LOW TIDE!" a helpful boater was shouting.

"Please," Paddy was saying, very quietly now.

"I think she's moving!" Captain Dan sang out.

In fact, the *Jersey Girl* was exhibiting no more flotation than central Nebraska. As I clung to the boom, listening to Paddy whimper, two thoughts penetrated my pain: (1) He was paying for this experience; and (2) If you have to die, you want it to be for a noble cause. You don't want it to be for Big Dick and the Extenders.

It turned out we didn't die. We finally got swung back onto the boat and began thinking about leading our lives without moving any muscles ever again. And eventually Captain Dan got the boat unstuck. He needed the help of a motorboat. I am certain this was also true of Columbus.

THE LIVING BRA

I had hoped that we could get the new year under way without any reports of ecologically dangerous shellfish attacking women's undergarments, but I see now that I was a fool.

I have here an alarming news article written by Christopher Taylor of the *Watertown* (New York) *Daily Times* and sent in by several alert readers. The headline, which I am not making up, says: LARGE COLONY OF ZEBRA MUSSELS FOUND CLINGING TO BIG BRASSIERE.

In case you haven't heard, the zebra mussel is a hot new environmental threat. Forget the killer bees. Oh, sure, they got a lot of scary headlines—KILLER BEES SIGHTED IN MEXICO; KILLER BEES SIGHTED IN TEXAS; KILLER BEES BECOME AMWAY DISTRIBUTORS—but they never lived up to their potential. Whereas at this very moment, the zebra mussel is raging out of control in the Great Lakes region. Well, OK, maybe "raging" is a strong term. As a rule, mussels don't rage. You rarely hear swimmers being advised: "If you see a mussel, try to remain calm, and whatever you do, *don't provoke it.*"

Nevertheless, we have reason to fear the zebra mussel, which gets its name from the fact that it roams the plains of Africa in giant herds.

No, seriously, it gets its name from the fact that it has a striped shell, which grows to about an inch long. About five years ago a group of zebra mussels, possibly carrying forged passports, came from Europe to the Great Lakes in the bilge water of a European ship, and they've been reproducing like crazy ever since. They are the Sex Maniacs of the Sea. Here's a quote from an August 1991 *Washington Post* article:

"Each female can produce 30,000 eggs a year, leading to huge colonies of billions of the animals clinging to every available surface. Recently, marine biologists have discovered concentrations reaching 700,000 mussels a cubic yard. . . .''

So apparently spaying them on an individual basis is out of the question. But something has to be done, because zebra mussels are clogging up water-supply pipes, and they're spreading fast. Controlling them could cost billions of dollars—money that will have to come out of the pockets of the scumballs who wrecked the savings-and-loan industry.

No! That was another joke! The money will of course come from lowlife taxpayers such as yourself, which is why you need to stay informed about this story, especially the giant-brassiere angle. Here are the key quotes from the *Watertown Daily Times* story:

> A large brassiere pulled from waters near the Genesee River at Rochester was carrying the largest colony of zebra mussels found so far in Lake Ontario. . . .
>
> The brassiere—and the mussels—are now under observation at the Department of Environmental Conservation Fisheries Research Station at Cape Vincent.
>
> DEC Supervisory Aquatic Biologist Gerard C. LeTendre said the bra was scooped up while DEC staff were trawling for dead lake trout near the Genesee River . . . Because of the size of the garment, Mr. LeTendre said, more than 100 mussels had managed to attach themselves to it.
>
> "Whoever that bra belonged to was of large proportions," Mr. LeTendre said. "It was huge."

This episode raises a number of troubling questions, including:

- They were trawling for *dead trout*?
- Is that sporting?
- Could it possibly be that the zebra mussels have become carniverous and *ate* the original bra occupant?
- Has anybody seen Dolly Parton *in person* recently?

In an effort to get to the bottom of this, I called the research station and grilled Gerard LeTendre.

"Is it true," I said, "that you have a large brassiere under observation?"

"It's really just in a box in my office," he said. "The newspaper made it sound like we have it in an aquarium."

He also said they still don't know who owns the bra.

"We know it's a four-hook bra," he said. "But it didn't belong to a large person. It was just a very well-endowed person."

He said that many people have offered suggestions about what to do with the bra, including "holding a Cinderella-type contest to see who it fits."

For now, however, the mystery remains unsolved. Meanwhile, the zebra mussels continue to multiply. Even as you read these words, a huge colony of them could be clustering ominously around a Sears catalog that fell overboard, nudging it open to the foundation-garments section. It is a chilling thought, and until the authorities come up with a plan of action, I am urging everybody to take the sensible precaution of developing a nervous facial tic. Also, if you *must* wear a brassiere, please wear it on the outside, where the Department of Environmental Conservation can keep an eye on it. Thank you.

READER ALERT

This section contains several true-life adventures, including the incident wherein Calvin Trillin and I came within inches of being savagely attacked by a dangerous and heavily armed criminal. Or possibly not. (I should note for the record that Trillin claims he acted much more heroically than the way he is depicted in this column; my feeling about that is, if he wants to appear heroic, he should write his own column about it.)

This section also contains the column I wrote about my first encounter with the world-famous Lawn Rangers precision lawnmower drill team of Arcola, Illinois. Since then I've returned to Arcola twice to march with this proud unit in the annual Broom Corn parade, a wonderful small-town, heartland event that features a tremendous outpouring of what can only be described as "beer."

CRIME BUSTERS

Somebody has got to do something about crime in the streets. Every day it seems as though there are more criminals running loose out there, and the quality of their work is *pathetic*.

I base this statement on a crime experience I had recently in the streets of New York City while visiting Calvin Trillin, who lives in New York and divides his time pretty much equally between being a well-known writer and trying to park his car. This experience, which I am not making up, occurred as we were returning to Calvin's house at about 1 A.M. after an evening of business-related nonpersonal tax-deductible literary research.

Just as we reached his door, a criminal appeared from out of the darkness and attempted to rob us. Up to that point, I have no criticism of the criminal's technique. He had done an excellent job of victim selection: In terms of physical courage, Calvin and I were probably the two biggest weenies abroad in Manhattan at that hour. A competent criminal, armed with any plausible weapon, including a set of nail clippers, could have had us immediately begging for mercy and handing over our wallets and promis-

144

ing to raise additional cash first thing in the morning by applying for second mortgages.

But this criminal had a terrible plan of action. He had both hands in his jacket pockets, and he was thrusting the jacket material out toward us, the way the bad guy's jacket sticks out on TV when he has a gun in his pocket and he doesn't want everybody to see it. Clearly Calvin and I were supposed to think that the criminal had two guns pointing at us.

Here's what the criminal said: "I'll blow both of your heads off."

Later on, in our detailed postcrime critique, Calvin and I found numerous flaws in this approach. For one thing,

if the criminal really *had* two guns, why on earth would he hide them? As Calvin pointed out: "You would definitely want to *show* your guns to a couple of schlubs like us."

Also, two guns was definitely overkill. According to my calculations, two guns figures out to one gun per hand, which raises the question: How was the criminal planning to take our wallets? Was he going to ask us to hold one of his guns for him? Was he going to have us stick the wallets in his mouth? If so, he would have had trouble giving us our postrobbery instructions, such as "Don't try following me!" or "Don't try anything funny!"

CRIMINAL (with his hands in his pockets and our wallets in his mouth): Donghh ghry angyghing ghunny!

ME: What?

CRIMINAL (getting angry): DONGHH GHRY ANGYGHING GHUNNY!

CALVIN: I think he's saying "Don't I have a big tummy."

ME (hastily): No! You're very svelte! Really! Sir!

But the criminal's silliest move, in my opinion, was threatening to blow both of our heads off. That would be an absurd waste of bullets. A much more efficient way to gain our cooperation would have been to simply blow *Calvin's* head off. I would then have cooperatively handed over Calvin's wallet.

So it was a very poorly planned robbery. I would like to say that Calvin and I, even as we were staring down the menacing barrels of the criminal's jacket pockets, instantly detected all the flaws with our computerlike brains. But frankly, due to the amount of literary research we had done that evening, our brains were not so much in computer mode as in Hubble Space Telescope mode, if you get my drift.

Nevertheless, I'm very proud of how we handled the situation. Actually, it was Calvin who took charge. You never really know what kind of gumption a man has, what kind of spine, what kind of plain old-fashioned "guts," until you see how he handles himself when the chips are down and all the marbles are on the line. Calvin looked at the criminal and he looked at me, and then, drawing on some inner reserve of strength and courage, he pressed the intercom button and said, "Alice, let us in."

Alice is Calvin's wife. She buzzed the door lock, and we opened the door and went inside, leaving the criminal out there with his jacket pockets still pointing at us. He never did blow our heads off, although the next morning I wished that he had.

Anyway, it was a pretty sorry performance, and if he is in any way representative of the criminals out there today, this is yet another area where the United States is heading down the tubes. I hope that the criminal, if he is reading this, has enough self-respect to learn from the criticisms I've outlined here and get his act together. Although in all fairness I should warn him that Calvin and I have given our performance some thought, and if this criminal ever tries to rob us again, he might be in for a little surprise. Because next time we're going to take strong, decisive action. Next time we're going to have Alice come out and give him a *piece of her mind*.

FALSE ALARM

The man was standing right outside our master bathroom. He couldn't see Beth and me, standing in the hallway, but we could see him clearly. His face was covered with a stocking mask, which distorted his features hideously. He was dressed all in black, and he had a black plastic bag stuck in his back pocket.

He was using a screwdriver to open our sliding glass door.

You always wonder what you're going to do in a situation like this. Run? Fight? Wet your pants?

I'm not experienced with physical violence. The last fight I had was in eighth grade, when I took on John Sniffen after school because he let the air out of my bike tires. Actually, I didn't *know* that he did this, but he was the kind of kid who *would* have, and all the other suspects were a lot larger than I was.

The man outside our house was also larger than I am. He jerked the screwdriver sideways and opened the door. Just like that, he was inside our house, maybe six feet from where Beth and I were standing.

Then he saw us. For a moment, nobody spoke.

"CUT!" yelled the director.

"Way to go, Ozzie!" I said to the stocking-masked man. "Looking good! Looking criminal!"

"I'm wondering if his bag is too dark to show up," said Beth.

Everybody wants to be a director.

Anyway, as you have guessed, Ozzie wasn't a real burglar. He was part of a production crew that was using our house to shoot a promotional video for the company that installed our burglar alarm. Here in South Florida it's standard procedure to have burglar alarms in your house, your car, your workplace, and, if you've had expensive dental work, your mouth.

I like having an alarm in our house, because it gives me the security that comes from knowing that trained security personnel will respond instantly whenever I trigger a false alarm. I do this every day at 6 A.M., when I get up to let out our large main dog, Earnest, and our small emergency-backup dog, Zippy. I'm always in a big hurry, because Zippy, being about the size of a hairy lima bean (although less intelligent), has a very fast digestive cycle, and I need to get him right outside.

So I fall out of bed, barely conscious, and stagger to the back door, where both dogs are waiting, and I open the door and *BWEEPBWEEPBWEEP* I realize that I have failed to disarm the alarm system.

Now I have a problem. Because, within seconds, the voice of the Cheerful Lady at the alarm company is going to come out of the alarm control panel, asking me to identify myself, and unless I give her the Secret Password, she's going to cheerfully notify the police. So I stagger quickly over to the panel. But this leaves Earnest and Zippy alone out on the patio. Theoretically, they can get from the patio to our backyard all by themselves. They used to be prevented from doing this by a screen enclosure around the patio, but thanks to Hurricane Andrew, most of this enclosure is now orbiting the Earth. The hurricane did NOT blow away the screen door, however. It's still standing there, and the dogs firmly believe that it's the only way out. So—I swear I'm not making this up—instead of going two feet to the left or right, where there's nothing to prevent them from simply wandering out into the yard, they trot directly to the door, stop, then turn around to look at me with a look that says "Well?"

"GO OUTSIDE!" I yell at them as I lunge toward the

alarm control panel. "THERE'S NO SCREEN ANYMORE, YOU MORONS!"

"I beg your pardon?" says the Cheerful Alarm Lady, because this is not the Secret Password.

"Bark," says Earnest, who is trotting back toward the house, in case I am telling her that it's time to eat.

"Grunt," says Zippy, as his internal digestive timer reaches zero and he detonates on the patio.

We do this almost every morning. We're very dependable. In fact, if some morning I DIDN'T trigger a false alarm, I think the Cheerful Alarm Lady would notify the police.

"You'd better check the Barry residence," she'd say. "Apparently something has happened to Mr. Barry. Or else he's strangling one of his dogs."

So the alarm people have been very nice to us, which is why we let them use our house for the video. It had a great Action Ending, wherein Ozzie runs out our front door, and an armed security man drives up, screeches to a halt, leaps out, puts his hand on his gun, and yells "FREEZE!" This is Ozzie's cue to freeze and look concerned inside his stocking. They shot this scene several times, so there was a lot of commotion in our yard. Fortunately, in South Florida we're used to seeing people sprint around with guns and stocking masks, so the activity in our yard did not alarm the neighbors. ("Look, Walter, the Barrys planted a new shrub." "Where?" "Over there, next to the burglar.") Anyway, the point is that our house is well protected. The alarm system is there in case we ever need it, which I doubt we will, because—thanks to Zippy—only a fool would try to cross our patio on foot.

THE WORLD'S FASTEST LAWN MOWER

When I hear some loudmouth saying that the United States is no longer a world technology leader, I look him in the eye and say: "Hey! There's a worm pooping on your shirt!" Then, when he looks down, I spit on the top of his head and sprint away. I'm not about to stand still while somebody knocks my country, not when we're still capable of achievements such as the World's Fastest Lawn Mower.

That's right: The World's Fastest Lawn Mower is produced right here in the U.S.A. by Americans just like yourself except that *you* are probably normal, whereas they put a jet-powered helicopter engine on a riding lawn mower. I know this is true because—call me a courageous journalism pioneer if you must—I drove it on my own personal lawn.

This event was arranged by Ken Thompson, a Miami-based sales representative for the Dixie Chopper brand of lawn mower. He wrote me a letter saying that the Dixie Chopper people had a special customized jet-powered model touring around the country making personal appearances, and it would be in my area, and he thought it would be a good idea if they brought it to my house in a sincere humanitarian effort to get free publicity. As a professional journalist trained to be constantly on the alert for stories that I can cover without leaving home, I said sure.

I've had an interest in lawn mowers since I was 10 years old, and I used to earn money by attempting to mow neighbors' lawns with our lawn mower, which was powered by the first gasoline engine ever built. I believe this was actually a stone engine. The only person who could start it consistently was my father, and he could do this only by wrapping the rope around the starter thing and

yanking it for the better part of the weekend, a process that required more time and energy than he would have expended if he'd cut the entire lawn with his teeth.

By about the 1,000th yank, he'd be dripping with sweat, ready to quit, and the lawn mower, sensing this, would go, and I quote: *Putt.* Just once. But that was enough to goad my father into a furious yanking frenzy, transforming himself, wolfmanlike, from a mild-mannered, gentle Presbyterian minister into a violent red-faced lunatic, yanking away at this malevolent stone, which continued to go *putt* at exactly the right tactical moment, until finally it got what it wanted, which was for my father to emit a burst of extremely mild profanity. Then the lawn mower, knowing that it now had a funny story to tell down at the Lawn Mower Bar, would start.

Sometimes, in an effort to earn money, I'd push the stone lawn mower next door and ask Mrs. Reed if she wanted me to mow her lawn. She'd say yes, and I'd yank on the starter thing for a while, then sit down, exhausted and discouraged, and Mrs. Reed, who had been watching from her kitchen, would come out and give me a quarter. It was a living.

Lawn mower technology has come a long way since then, as I discovered when the Dixie Chopper trailer pulled up at my house and the crew wheeled out the World's Fastest Lawn Mower. It's a normal-looking commercial riding lawn mower except that it has what looks like a large industrial coffee-maker mounted horizontally on the back. This is a 150-horsepower turbine engine from a U.S. military Chinook helicopter. According to the crew, Warren Evans and Mark Meagher, it can easily make the lawn mower go more than 60 miles per hour. God alone knows what it could do in a Cuisinart.

After briefing me on the controls, the crew started the

engine, which sounded like a giant vacuum cleaner, getting louder and louder like this: *whooOOOMMMM* until it was shrieking and shooting flames out the back and causing all the wildlife creatures in South Florida to start fleeing north, which is fine with me because most of them sting, anyway. Then I put on some ear protectors, climbed into the driver's seat, pushed the controls forward, and WHOOOAAAAA . . .

Let me say, in all journalistic objectivity, that I have never before experienced that level of acceleration in a lawn mower, or for that matter a commercial aircraft. Rocketing around my yard, watching concerned Dixie Chopper people leap out of the way, I was thinking: This is GREAT! I want to take this baby out on the INTERSTATE! I want to . . . *WHUMP*.

OK, so I hit a tree. But the mower was undamaged, and so was I, and the tree is expected to recover. The bottom line is, if you're interested in extremely high-speed lawn care, this is the lawn mower for you. The Dixie Chopper people said they'll make one for you just like it for only $29,000, which, according to my calculations, you could easily earn by simply not mowing Mrs. Reed's lawn 116,000 times.

WHO *WAS* THAT MASKED MAN?

Recently I had the honor of marching with the world-renowned Lawn Ranger precision power lawn-mower drill team at the famous Arcola Broom Corn Festival.

Just in case you never heard of this famous event, let me explain that Arcola is a town in Illinois, just north of Mattoon. Arcola (slogan: "Amazing Arcola") claims the proud distinction of having formerly been "one of the nation's top producers of broom corn, the primary ingredient in brooms." The town is still a major power in the broom industry.

Each September Arcola holds the Broom Corn Festival, featuring, among other events, a parade. For 11 years one of the key marching units has been the Lawn Rangers, who are considered by many observers who have had a couple of beers to be the finest precision lawn-mower drill team in the world.

When the Rangers invited me to march this year, I accepted eagerly, although I was concerned about being able to live up to the unit's high standards, as explained in this excerpt from the official Ranger newsletter, written by Ranger co-founder Pat Monahan:

The Lawn Ranger
and his faithful
companion,
TORO.

"As always, we will be living our motto, 'You're only young once, but you can always be immature.' This is a fine motto, but it can be carried to excess. Here I am thinking of Pee-wee Herman."

On the day of the parade, Monahan picked me up at the Champaign, Illinois, airport and drove me through large quantities of agriculture to Arcola. In addition to some nice grain elevators, Arcola boasts the nation's largest collection of antique brooms and brushes, as well as an establishment called the French Embassy, which is a combination gourmet restaurant and 12-lane bowling alley. I swear I am not making any of this up.

En route, Monahan explained the philosophy of the Lawn Rangers, which is that it is possible for a group of truly dedicated men to have a lot of fun yet at the same time do absolutely nothing useful for society. The Rangers' arch-enemy marching organization is the Shriners, who engage in worthwhile activities and are therefore regarded by the Rangers as being dangerously responsible.

Ranger Orientation took place in the garage of Ranger Ted Shields. About 50 Rangers were gathered around a keg, engaging in intensive mental preparation as well as "shanking," which is when you sneak up behind somebody and yank down his shorts. Next we had the annual business meeting, which I can't describe in a family newspaper except to say that at one point a Ranger, using a strategically placed ear of corn, gave a dramatic interpretation of the song "Shine On, Harvest Moon" that will haunt me for the rest of my life.

Then it was time for Rookie Camp. We rookies were each given a power lawn mower and a broom and told to line up on the street, where we received intensive instruction in precision-drill maneuvers.

"LISTEN UP, YOU GRAVY-SUCKERS!" shouted our Column Leaders, who carried long-handled toilet plungers to denote their rank. "ALL MANEUVERS WILL START WITH THE BROOMS-UP POSITION! THE BROOMS WILL ALWAYS COME UP ON THE CURB SIDE!"

We learned two maneuvers: Walking the Dog, which is when you hold your broom up while turning your lawn mower in a circle; and Cross and Toss, which is when you cross paths with another Ranger, then each of you tosses his broom to the other. These maneuvers require great precision, and we rookies were forced to train in the grueling sun for nearly two full minutes before we could perform them to the Rangers' exacting standards.

Finally it was time to march. We formed two columns,

each of us wearing a cowboy hat and a Lone Ranger–style mask. We were pushing a wide variety of customized lawn mowers, one of which had a toilet mounted on it. As we neared the main parade street, we stopped, gathered together, and put our hands into a huddle, where Monahan delivered an inspirational speech that beautifully summed up the meaning of Rangerhood:

"Remember," he said, "you guys are NOT SHRIN-ERS."

Thus inspired, we turned down the parade route, went to the brooms-up position, and executed the Cross and Toss with total 100 percent flawless perfection except for a couple of guys dropping their brooms. Some onlookers were so awed by this electrifying spectacle that they almost fell down.

When it was over I stood with my fellow Rangers, engaging in further mental preparation and accepting the compliments of the public ("Do you guys have *jobs?*"). At that moment I knew that I was part of something special, something important, something that someday, I hope, can be controlled by medication. But until then, Amazing Arcola, Illinois, will serve as a shining example of why America is what it is. Whatever that may be.

━━━━━ READER ALERT ━━━━━

This section is about music. It starts with a semiserious piece about Elvis and the mystery of why his fans feel as deeply about him as they do. It then moves to my experience in the Rock Bottom Remainders, a group of authors who discovered that, even though they had very little musical training, they were nevertheless able, with a little practice and a lot of heart, to turn themselves into a profoundly mediocre band.

Speaking of bad music: This section also presents the results of my Bad Song Survey, which attracted more mail than anything else I've ever written. People are *still* writing to tell me how much they hate, for example, "Running Bear." As you read this section, please bear in mind that the survey is *over*, OK? We already have our winners, so there is *no need to write to me*. Just read the results and get the bad songs stuck inside your brain so you can quietly hum them over and over until you go insane. Thank you.

HEARTS THAT ARE TRUE

When he was alive, they lived at the gates of Graceland.

It didn't matter whether he was there or not. They'd go, anyway, to be with each other, to talk about him, to be close to the place he loved. If he was there, they'd synchronize their lives with his: sleeping by day, when he slept, so they could be at the gates at night, in case he came out.

Sometimes he'd just drive by, on a motorcycle or in one of his spectacular cars, waving, and they'd try to follow him, and it might turn into an elaborate motorized game of hide-and-seek on the roads around Memphis. Sometimes he and his entourage, his guys, would be having one of their fireworks fights, and they'd roar down and attack the gate regulars, scaring them, thrilling them. And sometimes he'd come down to the gate and talk, sign autographs, get his picture taken, just *be* with them. Those were the best times, although they didn't happen much near the end.

Some of the gate people had jobs, but only so they could afford food and a place to sleep. Their real job, their purpose, was to be at the gates. They helped the guards—who knew them well—keep an eye on the wild fans, the nonregulars, who sometimes tried to get up to the front door.

"We were really his best security," says Linda Cullum, "because we would have killed anybody who we thought would have done anything to him."

Cullum arrived in 1964. She was in the Navy, and she had asked to be stationed in Memphis. "I didn't even know if they had a base here," she says. "I just knew he was here." She's 44 now, and she still lives nearby, as do others who were drawn to the gates in the good times. But they rarely go there anymore. These days the gates are for tourists: standing out front, getting their pictures taken, smiling the same way they'd smile in front of any other tourist attraction. You don't see it in their eyes, the thing that haunts the eyes of the gate people, the shining sweet sadness, the burning need that still consumes 10 years after they lost him.

"I still feel like I need to protect him," says Cullum. "Because, you know, there's so much you hear, so much that people say . . ."

Elvis fans. A species unto themselves. A large species. The ones like Linda Cullum, the gate people, are among the most dedicated, but there are a lot more, counting the ones—and, believe me, they are all around you—who don't talk about it. Because you might laugh. Because you don't understand.

These are not people who merely *liked* Elvis. A lot of us liked Elvis, especially when he was lean and sexy and strange and really bothered people. But then we moved on to the Beatles and the Stones and a lot of other (to us) hipper people, and Elvis, getting less scary and less lean all the time, faded into a '50s memory, and eventually he became, to many, a sad joke.

But don't laugh too soon, hip people. Think about this: *Over a billion* Elvis records have been sold. Nobody is in second place. And think about this: Today—10 years after he died, more than 20 years after he dominated rock— there are *tens of thousands* of people, from all over the world, gathered in Memphis to pay tribute to him, to visit Graceland, to walk the halls of his old high school, to take bus trips down to his Mississippi birthplace, to relive and explore and discuss and celebrate every tiny detail of his life. It isn't a one-time thing: The fans were there last year, and they'll be there next year. This doesn't happen for the Beatles; it doesn't happen for Frank Sinatra; it doesn't happen for Franklin D. Roosevelt. It doesn't happen for *anybody,* that I can think of, who is not the focal point of a major religion.

Just Elvis. Bruce Springsteen comes and Michael Jackson goes, but Elvis *endures.* His fans, his vast, quiet flock, make damn sure of that. They have heard all the stories about him, all the exposés and the Shocking Revelations about his appetites, his kinkiness, his temper, his pills. They know all about his problems. They know more about them than you do. And it makes no difference, except maybe to make them love him more, the way you draw closer, in time of trouble, to a brother or a lover. Which is what Elvis was to them. Which he still is.

And the hell with what people say.

The fans know what their public image is, too: fat, weeping, heavily hair-sprayed, middle-aged housewives wearing polyester pantsuits festooned with "I ♥ Elvis" buttons. That's all that gets on TV, the fans say. That's all the press sees.

"Ah, the press," sighs Karen Loper, 42, president of the

Houston-based Because of Elvis fan club. She was watching the Iran-contra hearings when I called her a couple of weeks ago. Like the other fan club presidents I talked to, she was very articulate. She does not wear polyester pantsuits.

''The media—especially the TV people—always do the obligatory story,'' she says. ''They pick the most unflattering person, the one with a black bouffant hairdo, and they show her at the graveside crying. It's so superficial, and nobody ever looks beyond it. But hey, I'm used to it. I've been putting up with this crap since I was 12 years old. First my father, always telling me Elvis wasn't gonna last, Elvis can't sing. Now the media. It used to bother me. I used to try to defend him. But now I realize: He doesn't need defending.''

This is a recurring theme with Elvis fans: They're tired of explaining themselves. If you don't hear what they hear, feel what they feel, that's your misfortune. If you want, they'll talk to you about it, but they don't expect you to understand.

Shirley Connell, 39, was one of the early gate people, back in the '60s. She had two big advantages:

1. Her family's backyard adjoins Graceland's.
2. Her mama loved Elvis, too.

Which meant young Shirley was allowed to spend virtually all her waking time, except for school, at the gates. And, like other regulars, she sometimes got invited along on the outings Elvis organized. Which is how it happened that one year she and her mama went to the movies all night, almost every night, from November through March.

Elvis regularly rented a downtown Memphis movie theater so he and his entourage could watch first-run movies (never his own, most of which embarrassed him). For years, his fans, the regulars, were allowed to join him. They weren't exactly *with* him, but they were in the same *room* with him, and that was enough.

"The schedule was," Connell recalls, "he'd come in, and we'd watch anywhere from three to five movies, and he'd leave. Then I'd go home, and if given enough time, I'd catch a nap, and if not, I'd go straight to school. Then I'd come home from school at 2:30 in the afternoon, do my homework, and go straight to bed. Then I'd get up at 10 o'clock and find out what time the movie was.

"We saw *The Nutty Professor* 14 times. *The Great Escape* was 10. *Doctor Strangelove* was 12. Mama would go to sleep. . . . I went out and ate one time, during *The Nutty Professor;* I couldn't stand it anymore. But I was just gone long enough to eat. I didn't *dare* leave."

If you ask her why, it shows you could never understand.

Connell still lives in the same modest ranch house. She has pictures of Elvis on the walls, and a lot of souvenirs, including one of Elvis's custom-made silk shirts and an RCA portable radio Elvis gave her for Christmas in 1963. She has the box, the wrapping paper, the original long-dead battery.

She took me out to her backyard one evening and dragged out a rickety old ladder so I could climb up and look over the wooden fence into the manicured grounds of Graceland. Two of Elvis's horses were grazing there. She hasn't looked over that fence in years.

Graceland today is a business, a tourist attraction operated by the Presley estate. The mansion, built in 1939, sits on a small hill overlooking Route 51, which in Memphis is Elvis Presley Boulevard. When Elvis, then 22, bought Graceland in 1957 for $100,000 the area was mostly country; now the boulevard is a semisleazy strip, lined with car dealerships and fast-food places. (Not that this is inappropriate, cars and fast food being two things Elvis consumed in vast quantities.)

Half a million people visit Graceland each year, but most of them are tourists, as opposed to True Fans. Most go for the same reason they would go to see a man wrestle an alligator: curiosity. Sure, they like Elvis, or they wouldn't be there. But when they go through the house, stand where he stood, look at the things he owned and touched, they're not *moved*. Some are even amused.

And, Lord knows, there is plenty to be amused about. The decor is stunningly, at times hilariously, tacky, representing the Let's-Not-Leave-a-Single-Square-Inch-Anywhere-Including-the-Ceiling-Undecorated school of interior design, featuring electric-blue drapes, veined wall mirrors, carpeting on the ceiling, etc. And it's hard not to laugh at the earnest speeches of the clean-cut, relentlessly perky young guides, describing, say, Elvis's collection of police badges, as though these were artifacts at Monticello.

Scene from the tour: We're in the TV room, which has mirrors on the ceiling and a squint-inducing navy-blue-with-bright-yellow color scheme. "You'll notice the three TVs in front of you," the guide says. "This is an idea Elvis got from Lyndon Johnson."

Now we're in an outbuilding, originally built for Elvis's extensive model-racing-car layout (which he quickly got bored with and gave away) and now housing a memorabilia display. We pause before a display of extravagantly overdecorated jumpsuit costumes. ". . . Elvis found the fringe to be a problem onstage," the guide is saying, "so he moved on to outfits that were more studded."

The tour ends when, in a bizarre juxtaposition, we move from Elvis's racquetball court to his grave, out by the swimming pool. This is where the True Fans often break down.

The tourists, though, usually just take pictures, then head back across the street to the plaza of stores selling licensed souvenirs. This is a place where good taste never even tries to rear its head. Just about anything they can put a likeness of Elvis on and sell, they do. You can get, for $295, a decanter shaped like Elvis wearing a karate uniform. You can get some Love Me Tender Conditioning Rinse. If you like to read, you can get a copy of *I Called Him Babe—Elvis Presley's Nurse Remembers*. You can get sick.

But here's the thing: the True Fans don't much like this, either. Most of them accept it, because they know that without the tourists and the souvenir dollars Graceland would have to close, and they'd lose a strong link with him. But they don't *like* it. They don't want a souvenir manufactured in Taiwan 10 years after Elvis died; they want something *real*.

Like Elvis's cigar butt. Tom Kirby got one. His friend and fellow gate regular, Debbie Brown, recalls how this came about:

"We were good friends with Jo Smith, who was married to Elvis's cousin, and she had always been real thoughtful, especially as far as Tom was concerned, because he had always been such a good fan. . . . So they were playing racquetball or something, and [Elvis] laid his cigar down, half smoked, and then he walked out. So she picked it up, and she thought it would be a real neat souvenir for Tom. So she brings this cigar to Tom—she wrapped it up in a little tinfoil paper—and Tom is so excited, he runs over in the middle of the night, pounds on the door, and I go, 'What,' and he says, 'Look what Jo's given me.' And he unwraps the precious little tinfoil holding his cigar, and he goes, 'God, Elvis's cigar. It's just fresh, she got it tonight.' And I go, 'God, let me see it.' And I grab it and stick it right in my mouth, because I know it's been in *his* mouth. And Tom goes, 'But I haven't even put it in *my* mouth yet!' "

An even more wonderful thing happened in Atlanta, where Brown, Kirby, and some other gate people went to see Elvis in concert, and where they managed to get into his actual hotel room, after he had left for his last show.

"The keys were hanging in the presidential suite, in the door," Brown recalls. "We instantly took the keys out, went inside, and shut the door. We went through the wastepaper cans. . . . We were running around, jerking open cabinets. There was a cart there, and it had a big giant urn of the most horrible black coffee—that's the way he liked his coffee—and the bacon there was on a large platter, and it was burned to a crisp—that's the way he ate his bacon. Instantly we knew we had success, and we just grabbed this bacon—*Elvis* had this!—and we went [she makes gobbling sounds]. You know, so we can say we ate with him. He just wasn't there, but we ate off his tray.

"Then my girlfriend and I looked at each other, and we thought—*the bed*! So I ripped the sheets back, and she said, 'What are you doing?' And I said, 'I'm looking!' And she said, 'For what?' I said, *'A pubic hair!'*

"You'd have to be a diehard fan to appreciate that. I mean, I know it sounds sick, but wouldn't that be the *ultimate,* for a female?"

I'm driving the 93 miles down Highway 78 from Memphis to Tupelo, Mississippi, where Elvis was born and lived for 13 years, to see if maybe I can get a clue as to what this is all about.

The drive feels very Rural Southern. Kudzu vines swarm everywhere. Corn is $1 a dozen. A preacher is talking on the radio.

"I've been down that Long Road of Sin," he says. "I went out and just *ate the world.*"

Election campaigns are under way, in the form of signs in people's yards.

RE-ELECT ZACK STEWART HIGHWAY COMMISSIONER

JIMMYE DALE GREEN SHERIFF

"Sometimes," the preacher says, "we all get in that old carnality way."

The Birthplace is at the end of a short street lined with extremely modest homes. Shacks, really. The Birthplace is a shack, too, only it has been fixed up nice and moved a short distance to a little park, which also has a modern building where you can buy souvenirs.

The Birthplace has only two rooms, furnished with donated items. The most authentic item there is Laverne Clayton, who sits in the bedroom and charges you $1 admission. She was born in 1935, same as Elvis; she lived next door to him for 10 years, went to school with him.

"He liked Karo syrup and butter and biscuits," she says. "He liked to play Roy Rogers. I was in the schoolroom, third grade, when he sang "Old Shep." We thought he was silly. We didn't pay him no mind."

And now she collects money from people who come from *Japan* just to see where he was born. And she doesn't understand, any more than I do, why.

"A lot of the people don't believe Elvis is dead," she says, shaking her head. "They tell me he's on an island somewhere.

"You don't argue with real Elvis fans. You just let them talk."

At the Birthplace I buy a book called *Elvis Now—Ours Forever*, a collection of reminiscences from True Fans edited by Bob Olmetti and Sue McCasland, who was a gate person in the mid-'70s. The book almost throbs in your hands with the intensity of the fans' devotion.

Jan Lancaster, Tupelo, Mississippi: "Every time I went to Memphis, I went by [Graceland]. . . . Like I was eight months pregnant, and my girlfriend and I went up there with our husbands. They went to a skin flick, dropped us off, and I had a coat on so if Elvis sees me he won't know I'm pregnant. We sat all night long—it was 22 degrees. . . ."

Linda Horr, Richmond, Indiana: "I don't think any fan could love Elvis as much as I do, except maybe, to the fans who have actually met him, the hurt is worse. If that is so, then I thank God for sparing me that kind of pain—for the loss I feel is bad enough."

Part of it, of course, is his music. He really *could* sing, and except for a sterile period in the '60s when he was acting in mostly awful movies with mostly awful soundtracks, he made a whole lot of good records—"Jailhouse Rock," "Heartbreak Hotel," "Suspicious Minds," "Burnin' Love," and many more that don't get played much on the radio. Elvis croons continuously over the P.A. system at the souvenir-store plaza across from Graceland, and as you wander around you often find yourself thinking when a new song comes on, Yeah, that was a pretty good one, too.

Part of it was his lack of pretense. I realize that seems like an odd way to talk about a pampered, insulated superstar who performed in spangled jumpsuits, but if you watch tapes of him in concert, what strikes you—what strikes me, anyway—is that, unlike his preening, pouting, self-important impersonators, the real Elvis never seemed to take himself particularly seriously. He laughed a lot, and most of his jokes were at his own expense—muttered throwaway lines about the legendary Pelvis, the Leer, and (near the end) the Paunch. He seemed to find the adulation as inexplicable as many of the rest of us do. Watching him, I found it hard not to like him.

"Elvis," says Linda Cullum, veteran of many years at the gates, "was always a regular person."

And indeed he was, in some ways. He got very famous, and he got very rich, but he didn't move to Monaco, didn't collect Matisse, didn't hang out with Society. He was a boy from the South, and he stayed in the South, and when he made it, he brought his daddy and mama and relatives and friends to live with him in and around his mansion. To the end, he hung out with good old boys, and he did the things a good old boy does, only more so.

There's a long-standing tradition in the American South in which getting drunk and/or stoned and chasing women and shooting off pistols and racing cars around for the sheer hell of it are normal, everyday male activities, generally accepted with a resigned or amused shrug by much of Southern society. In the show business part of this society they called this "roarin' with the 'billies [hillbillies]." In country music, tradition practically dictated that as soon as you got a little money, you went out and spent it on cars, clothes, rings and women, all flashy. Many in rock and roll adhered to this self-indulgent philosophy.

Elvis was a product of this culture and when you traveled with Elvis, you were roarin' with the No. 1 Billy.

—*Elvis: the Final Years,* by Jerry Hopkins

The cars, the guns, the jewelry, the wild parties, the binges, the famous plane trip from Memphis to Denver in the dead of night solely to buy peanut butter sandwiches— none of this bothers the fans. *Hey, it was his money. He earned it.*

Another part of it—a big part, the shrinks say—is sexual: repressed longings released by this exotic, sensual stud

171

who dared to thrust his hips at the Wonder Bread world that was white American pop culture in the '50s. But that was a long time ago, and there have been plenty of sex symbols since. Why do these people remain so loyal to Elvis? Why does it seem as though their ardor has intensified, rather than cooled, since his death?

And why are their feelings so *personal*, for a man some of them never saw in person, and many of them never met? Talk to a True Fan, and odds are she won't talk about Elvis's art, his *genius*, the way fans of, say, Bob Dylan will talk. Odds are she'll tell you how, when he performed, he always seemed to be looking at *her*, singing to *her*. The True Fans really believe that Elvis loved them, just as much as they love him. They talk about how much he cared for them, how much he gave them, how, in a way, *he died for them*. He was under so much pressure, the True Fans say; he worked so hard to meet the demands of his public. No wonder he was sick. No wonder he turned to drugs. In some fans you sense a distinct undercurrent of guilt: *If only he hadn't kept his pain so private; if only I had known, maybe I could have helped. . . .*

This devotion gets more and more confusing the longer I try to understand it. I've been reading books, listening to records, watching tapes, talking to fans, talking to Graceland officials. I have two notebooks full of quotes from people trying to explain the Elvis Thing. They can't, and neither can I.

But I'm not laughing at it, the way I used to.

There's a painful scene near the end of the documentary "This Is Elvis" showing Elvis in one of his final concerts, six weeks before he died. His appearance is shocking: This is a bloated, obviously sick man, his belly hanging out over the gaudy belt of his jumpsuit. He sings "Are You Lonesome Tonight," and when he gets to the talking part in the middle, he forgets the words; *forgets the words* to a song he must have sung a thousand times. He keeps going, stumbling and slurring, not looking at the audience, giggling to himself as he blows line after line, finally giving up.

When, mercifully, the song ends, Elvis introduces his father, Vernon, who looks only slightly older than his son, and much healthier. And then Elvis sings "My Way," holding a piece of paper, in case he forgets the words.

"Sometimes," says Debbie Brown, "I'll drive by the gates at about 3 in the morning—that was *his* time—and I'll turn my back on all the souvenir stores, and just look at the house, and it reminds me a little bit of what it was like. But I don't really like to do that too much, because it reminds me of how empty it is now. It's over. The fantasy's over.

"But just for a little time, I was part of something special. And *I* was special."

After Shirley Connell let me look over her back fence at Elvis's horses, she showed me her photo album. It's thick with snapshots of Elvis, many taken at the gates. Sometimes it's just Elvis; sometimes she's in the background; sometimes he has his arm around her. The two of them change, as you flip through the pages, he from bad-ass motorcycle rocker to Vegas headliner, she from girl to woman, the two of them growing older together.

"I try not to even drive by the gates anymore," she says.

NOW THAT'S SCARY

Recently I played lead guitar in a rock band, and the rhythm guitarist was—not that I wish to drop names—Stephen King. This actually happened. It was the idea of a woman named Kathi Goldmark, who formed a band consisting mostly of writers to raise money for literacy by putting on a concert at the American Booksellers Association convention in Anaheim, California.

So she called a bunch of writers who were sincerely interested in literacy and making an unbelievable amount of noise. Among the others who agreed to be in the band were Tad Bartimus, Roy Blount, Jr., Michael Dorris, Robert Fulghum, Matt Groening, Barbara Kingsolver, Ridley Pearson, and Amy Tan.

I think we all said yes for the same reason. If you're a writer, you sit all day alone in a quiet room trying to craft sentences on a word processor, which makes weenie little clickety-click sounds. After years and years of crafting and clicking, you are naturally attracted to the idea of arming yourself with an amplified instrument powerful enough to be used for building demolition, then getting up on a stage with other authors and screaming out songs such as "Land of 1,000 Dances," the lyrics to which express the following literary theme:

> Na, na na na na, na na na na
> Na na na, na na na, na na na na

So we all met in Anaheim, and for three days we rehearsed in a Secret Location under the strict supervision of our musical director, the legendary rock musician Al Kooper. This was a major thrill for me, because Kooper had been my idol when I was at Haverford College in the late 1960s. Back then I played guitar in a band called The

Federal Duck, and we tried very hard to sound like a band Al Kooper was in called The Blues Project. Eventually The Federal Duck actually made a record album, which was so bad that many stereo systems chose to explode rather than play it.

Anyway, I could not quite believe that, 25 years later, I was really and truly in a band with *Al Kooper,* and that he was actually asking for *my opinion* on musical issues. "Do you think," he would ask, "that you could play in the same key as the rest of us?"

So, OK, skillwise I'm not Eric Clapton. But I was *louder* than Eric Clapton, as well as many nuclear tests. I had an amplifier large enough to serve as public housing. It had a little foot switch, and when I pressed it, I was able to generate sound waves that will affect the global climate for years to come. We can only hope that Saddam Hussein is not secretly developing a foot switch like this.

We practiced six long hours the first day, and at the end, Al Kooper called us together for an inspirational talk.

"When we started this morning, we stunk," he said. "But by this afternoon, we stunk much better. Maybe eventually we can be just a faint odor."

In the evenings we engaged in literary activities such as going to see the movie *Alien³*. I was concerned about this, because when I watch horror movies I tend to whimper and clutch the person sitting next to me, who in this particular case was Stephen King. But as it turned out, the alien didn't scare me at all; I live in Miami, and we have cockroaches that are at least that size, but more aggressive. The only scary part was when Sigourney Weaver got injected with a hypodermic needle, which on the movie screen was approximately 27 feet long. This caused me to whimper and clutch Stephen King, but I was pleased to note that *he* was whimpering and clutching his wife, Tabitha.

But the real thrill came when our band finished practicing and actually played. The performance was in a big dance hall called the Cowboy Boogie, where hundreds of booksellers and publishing-industry people had drunk themselves into a highly literary mood. The show went great. The audience whooped and screamed and threw underwear. Granted, some of it was extra-large men's jockey briefs, but underwear is underwear. We belted out our songs, singing, with deep concern for literacy in our voices, such lyrics as:

> *You got to do the mammer jammer*
> *If you want my love.*

Also a group of rock critics got up with us and sang a version of "Louie Louie" so dirty that the U.S. Constitution should, in my opinion, be modified specifically to prohibit it.

Also—so far this is the highlight of my life—I got to play a lead-guitar solo while dancing the Butt Dance *with Al Kooper.* To get an idea how my solo sounded, press the following paragraph up against your ear:

BWEEEOOOOOAAAAPPPPPP

Ha ha! Isn't that *great?* Your ear is bleeding.

MUSTANG DAVEY

Recently, I was chosen to serve as a musical consultant to the radio industry.

Actually, it wasn't the entire industry; it was a woman named Marcy, who called me up at random one morning while I was picking my teeth with a business card as part of an ongoing effort to produce a column.

"I'm not selling anything," Marcy said.

Of course when callers say this, they usually mean that they ARE selling something, so I was about to say "No thank you" in a polite voice, then bang the receiver down with sufficient force to drive phone shards deep into Marcy's brain, when she said she was doing a survey for the radio industry about what songs should be played on the air.

That got my attention, because radio music is an issue I care deeply about. I do a lot of singing in the car. You should hear Aretha Franklin and me perform our version of "I Say a Little Prayer for You," especially when our voices swoop way up high for the ending part that goes, "My darling BELIEVE me, for me there is nooo WAHHHHH-AAANNNN but you" . . . My technique is to

178

grip the steering wheel with both hands and lift myself halfway out of the seat so that I can give full vocal expression to the emotion that Aretha and I are feeling, which is a mixture of joyous hope and bittersweet longing and the horror of realizing that the driver of the cement truck three feet away is staring at me, at which point I pretend that I am having a coughing seizure while Aretha finishes the song on her own.

I think they should play that song more often on the radio, along with "Brown-Eyed Girl," "Sweet Home Alabama," and of course the Isley Brothers' version of "Twist and Shout," which, if you turn it up loud enough, can propel you beyond mere singing into the stage where you have to get out of the car and dance with tollbooth attendants.

On the other hand, it would not trouble me if the radio totally ceased playing ballad-style songs by Neil Diamond. I realize that many of you are huge Neil Diamond fans, so let me stress that in matters of musical taste, everybody is entitled to an opinion, and yours is wrong. Consider the song "I Am, I Said," wherein Neil, with great emotion, sings:

> *I am, I said*
> *To no one there*
> *And no one heard at all*
> *Not even the chair.*

What kind of line is that? Is Neil telling us he's *surprised* that the chair didn't hear him? Maybe he expected the chair to say, "Whoa, I heard THAT." My guess is that Neil was really desperate to come up with something to rhyme with "there," and he had already rejected "So I ate a pear," "Like Smokey the Bear," and "There were nits in my hair."

So we could do without this song. I also believe that we should use whatever means are necessary—and I do not exclude tactical nuclear weapons—to prevent radio stations from ever playing "Honey," "My Way," "I Write the Songs," "I Never Promised You a Rose Garden," and "Watchin' Scotty Grow." I have holes in my car radio from stabbing the station-changing button when these songs come on. Again, you may disagree with me, but if you know so much, how come the radio industry didn't randomly survey *you?*

The way the survey worked was, Marcy played two-second snippets from about two dozen songs; after each snippet I was supposed to say whether I liked the song or not. She'd play, for example, "Don't Worry, Baby" by the Beach Boys and I'd shout "YES! PLAY THE WHOLE THING!" and she'd say, "OK, that's a 'like.' Or she'd play "Don't You Care" by the Buckinghams, and I'd make a noise like a person barfing up four feet of intestine, and Marcy would say, "OK, that's a 'don't like.' "

The problem was that I wasn't allowed to *suggest* songs. I could only react to the generally mediocre candidates that were presented. It was just like the presidential elections. This is too bad, because there are a lot of good songs that never get played. My wife and I are constantly remarking on this. I'll say, "Do you remember a song called 'Boys'?" And Beth, instantly, will respond, "Bop shoo-bop, boppa boppa SHOO-bop." Then both of us, with a depth of emotion that we rarely exhibit when discussing world events, will say, "They NEVER play that!"

I tried suggesting a couple of songs to Marcy. For example, after she played the "Don't Worry, Baby" snippet, I said, "You know there's a great Beach Boys song that never gets played called "Custom Machine." The chorus goes:

> *Step on the gas, she goes WAA-AAA-AAHH*
> *I'll let you look*
> *But don't touch my custom machine!*

I did a good version of this, but Marcy just went "Huh" and played her next snippet, which was "I Go to Pieces" by a group that I believe is called Two British Weenies. I don't care for that song, and I told Marcy as much, but I still keep hearing it on the radio. Whereas I have yet to hear "Custom Machine." It makes me wonder if the radio industry really cares what I think, or if I'm just a lonely voice crying out, and nobody hears me at all. Not even the chair.

THE WHAMMIES

In a recent column I noted that certain songs are always getting played on the radio, despite the fact that these songs have been shown, in scientific laboratory tests, to be bad. One example I cited was Neil Diamond's ballad "I Am, I Said," in which Neil complains repeatedly that nobody hears him, "not even the chair." I pointed out that this does not make a ton of sense, unless Neil has unusually intelligent furniture. ("Mr. Diamond, your BarcaLounger is on line two.")

Well, it turns out there are some major Neil Diamond fans out there in Readerland. They sent me a large pile of hostile mail with mouth froth spewing out of the envelope seams. In the interest of journalistic fairness, I will summarize their main arguments here:

Dear Pukenose:
   Just who the hell do you think you are to blah blah a great artist like Neil blah blah more than 20 gold records blah blah how many gold records do YOU have, you scumsucking wad of blah blah I personally

have attended 1,794 of Neil's concerts blah blah What about "Love on the Rocks"? Huh? What about "Cracklin' Rosie"? blah blah if you had ONE-TENTH of Neil's talent blah blah so I listened to "Heart Light" 40 times in a row and the next day the cyst was GONE and the doctor said he had never seen such a rapid blah blah. What about "Play Me"? What about "Song Sung Blah"? Cancel my subscription, if I have one.

So we can clearly see that music is a matter of personal taste. Person A may hate a particular song, such as "Havin' My Baby" by Paul Anka (who I suspect is also Neil Sedaka), and Person B might love this song. But does this mean that

Person B is wrong? Of course not. It simply means that Person B is an idiot. Because some songs are just plain bad, and "Havin' My Baby" is one of them, and another one is "Bad, Bad Leroy Brown."

That's not merely my opinion: That's the opinion of many readers who took time out from whatever they do, which I hope does not involve operating machinery, to write letters containing harsh remarks about these and other songs. In fact, to judge from the reader reaction, the public is a lot more concerned about the issue of song badness than about the presidential election campaign (which by the way is over, so you can turn on your TV again).

And it's not just the public. It's also the media. I put a message on the *Miami Herald*'s computer system, asking people to nominate the worst rock song ever, and within minutes I was swamped with passionate responses. And these were from *newspaper people,* who are legendary for their cold-blooded noninvolvement ("I realize this is a bad time for you, Mrs. Weemer, but could you tell me how you felt when you found Mr. Weemer's head?"). Even the managing editor responded, arguing that the worst rock song ever was "whichever one led to the second one."

Other popular choices were "A Horse with No Name," performed by America; "Billy, Don't Be a Hero," by Bo Donaldson and the Heywoods; "Kung Fu Fighting," by Carl Douglas; "Copacabana," by Barry Manilow; "Me and You and a Dog Named Boo," by Lobo; "Seasons in the Sun," by Terry Jacks; "Feelings," by various weenies; "Precious and Few" by some people who make the weenies who sang "Feelings" sound like Ray Charles; "The Pepsi Song," by Ray Charles; "Muskrat Love," by The Captain and Tennille; every song ever recorded by Bobby Goldsboro; and virtually every song recorded since about 1972.

"It's worse than ever" is how my wife put it.

Anyway, since people feel so strongly about this issue, I've decided to conduct a nationwide survey to determine the worst rock song ever. I realize that similar surveys have been done before, but this one will be unique: This will be the first rock-song survey ever, to my knowledge, that I'll be able to get an easy column out of.

So I'm asking you to consider two categories: Worst Overall Song and Worst Lyrics. In the second category, for example, you might want to consider a song I swear I heard back in the late 1950s, which I believe was called "Girls Grow Up Faster Than Boys Do." I've been unable to locate the record, but the chorus went:

> Won't you take a look at me now
> You'll be surprised at what you see now
> I'm everything a girl should be now
> Thirty-six, twenty-four, thirty-FIVE!

I'm sure you can do worse than that.

Send your card today. Be in with the "in" crowd. We'll have joy, we'll have fun. So Cracklin' Rosie, get on board, because Honey, I miss you. AND your dog named Boo.

THE WORST SONGS
EVER RECORDED

BAD SONG SURVEY

P ART O NE

Before I present the results of the Bad Song Survey, here's an important BRAIN TAKEOVER ALERT:

Be advised that this column names certain songs that you hate and have tried to suppress, but as soon as you read their names your brain will start singing "Yoouunngg girl, get out of my mind; my love for you is way out of line" . . . over and over AND YOU CAN'T STOP IT AIEEEEEEE. Thank you.

First, I have NEVER written a column that got a bigger response than the one announcing the Bad Song Survey. Over 10,000 readers voted, with cards still coming in. Also, wherever I went people expressed their views to me, often gripping my shirt to emphasize their points. ("You know that song about piña coladas? I hate that song. I HATE IT!") Song badness is an issue that Americans care deeply about.

Second, you Neil Diamond fans out there can stop writ-

ing irate unsigned letters telling me that I am not worthy to be a dandruff flake on Neil's head, OK? (Not that I am saying Neil has dandruff.) Because you have convinced me: Neil Diamond is GOD. I no longer see anything but genius in the song where he complains that his chair can't hear him. Unfortunately, a lot of survey voters are not so crazy about Neil's work, especially the part of "Play Me" where he sings:

> . . . *song she sang to me,*
> *song she brang to me* . . .

Of course *I* think those lyrics are brilliant; however, they brang out a lot of hostility in the readers. But not as much as "Lovin' You," sung by Minnie Riperton, or

"Sometimes When We Touch," sung by Dan Hill, who sounds like he's having his prostate examined by Captain Hook.

Many people still deeply resent these songs. Many others would not rule out capital punishment for anyone convicted of having had anything to do with Gary Puckett and the Union Gap ("Woman," "Young Girl," and "This Girl Is a Woman Now," which some voters argue are all the same song).

Likewise there are boiling pools of animosity out there for Barry "I Write the Songs" Manilow, Olivia "Have You Never Been Mellow" Newton-John, Gilbert "Alone Again, Naturally" O'Sullivan, The Village "YMCA" People, Tony "Knock Three Times" Orlando, and of course Yoko "Every Song I Ever Performed" Ono. And there is no love lost for the Singing Nun.

The voters are ANGRY. A typical postcard states: "The number one worst piece of pus-oozing, vomit-inducing, camel-spitting, cow-phlegm rock song EVER in the history of the SOLAR system is 'Dreams of the Everyday Housewife.' " (Amazingly, this song was NOT performed by Gary Puckett and the Union Gap.)

Here are some other typical statements:

—"I'd rather chew a jumbo roll of tinfoil than hear 'Hey Paula' by Paul and Paula."
—"Whenever I hear the Four Seasons' 'Walk Like a Man,' I want to scream, 'Frankie, SING like a man!' "
—"I wholeheartedly believe that 'Ballerina Girl' is responsible for 90 percent of the violent crimes in North America today."
—"I nominate every song every sung by the Doobie Brothers. Future ones also."

—"Have you noticed how the hole in the ozone layer has grown progressively larger since rap got popular?"

Sometimes the voters were so angry that they weren't even sure of the name of the song they hated. There were votes against "These Boots Are Made for Stomping"; the Beach Boys' classic "Carolina Girls"; "I'm Nothing But a Hound Dog"; and "Ain't No Woman Like the One-Eyed Gott." A lot of people voted for "The Lion Sleeps Tonight," offering a variety of interpretations of the chorus, including: "Weem-o-wep," "Wee-ma-wack," "Weena-wack," "A-ween-a-wap," and "Wingle whip."

Many readers are still very hostile toward the song "Wildfire," in which singer Michael Murphy wails for what seems like 97 minutes about a lost pony. (As one voter put it: "Break a leg, Wildfire.") Voter Steele Hinton particularly criticized the verse wherein *there came a killing frost,* which causes Wildfire to get lost. As Hinton points out: ". . . 'killing' in 'killing frost' refers to your flowers and your garden vegetables, and when one is forecast you should cover your tomatoes . . . Nobody ever got lost in a killing frost who wouldn't get lost in July as well."

There was also a solid vote for Gordon Lightfoot's "The Wreck of the Edmund Fitzgerald," a real fun party song. Several voters singled out the line: "As the big freighters go, it was bigger than most."

Speaking of bad lyrics, there were votes for:

—Cream's immortal "I'm So Glad," which eloquently expresses the feeling of being glad, as follows: "I'm so glad! I'm so glad! I'm glad, I'm glad, I'm glad!" (Repeat one billion times.)

—"La Bamba," because the lyrics, translated, are: "I am not a sailor. I am a captain, I am a captain, I am a captain." And he is probably glad.

189

—"Johnny Get Angry," performed by Joanie Sommers, who sings: "Johnny get angry, Johnny get mad; Give me the biggest lecture I ever had; I want a BRAVE man, I want a CAVE man . . ."

—"Take the Money and Run," in which Steve Miller attempts to rhyme "Texas" with "what the facts is," not to mention "hassle" with "El Paso."

—"Torn Between Two Lovers." (Reader comment: "Torn, yes, hopefully on the rack.")

—"There Ain't Enough Room in My Fruit of the Looms to Hold All My Love for You." (This might not be a real song, but I don't care.)

Certainly these are all very bad songs, but the scary thing is: *Not one song I've named so far is a winner.* I'll name the winners next week, after your stomach has settled down. Meanwhile, here are some more songs you should NOT think about: "Baby I'm-a Want You," "Candy Man," "Disco Duck," "I Am Woman," "Itsy-Bitsy Teeny-Weeny Yellow Polka-Dot Bikini," "Last Kiss," "Patches," "The Night Chicago Died," "My Ding-a-Ling," and "My Sharona." Just FORGET these songs. Really.

P.S. Also "Horse with No Name."

AND THE WINNER IS . . .

BAD SONG SURVEY

PART TWO

I hope you haven't had anything to eat recently, because, as promised last week, today I am presenting the winners of the Bad Song Survey.

In analyzing these results, I had to make a few adjustments. For example, the Bob Dylan song "Lay Lady Lay" would have easily won as Worst Overall Song, with 17,006 votes, except that I had to disallow 17,004 votes on the grounds that they were cast by my Research Department, Judi Smith, who tabulated the votes and who HATES "Lay Lady Lay."

To win, a song had to be known well enough so that a lot of people could hate it. This is a shame in a way, because some obscure songs that people voted for are wonderfully hideous. One reader sent a tape of a song called "Hooty Sapperticker," by a group called Barbara and the Boys. This could be the worst song I've ever heard. It consists almost entirely of the Boys singing "Hooty! Hooty! Hooty!" and then Barbara saying: "Howdy Hooty Sapperticker!"

Several readers sent in an amazing CD from Rhino Records called *Golden Throats,* which consists of popular actors attempting to sing popular music, including William Shatner attempting "Lucy in the Sky with Diamonds," Leonard Nimoy attempting "Proud Mary," Mae West attempting "Twist and Shout," Eddie Albert attempting "Blowin' in the Wind," and—this is my favorite—Jack "Mr. Soul" Webb attempting "Try a Little Tenderness." You need this CD.

But now for our survey results. Without question, the voters' choice for Worst Song—in both the Worst Overall AND Worst Lyrics category—is . . . (drum roll . . .)

"MacArthur Park," as sung by Richard Harris, and later remade, for no comprehensible reason, by Donna Summer.

It's hard to argue with this selection. My 12-year-old son Rob was going through a pile of ballots, and he asked me how "MacArthur Park" goes, so I sang it, giving it my best shot, and Rob laughed so hard that when I got to the part about leaving the cake out in the rain, and it took so long to bake it, and I'll never have that recipe again, Rob was on the *floor*. He didn't BELIEVE those lyrics were real. He was SURE his wacky old humor-columnist dad was making them up.

The clear runner-up, again in both categories, is "Yummy Yummy Yummy (I Got Love in My Tummy)," performed by Ohio Express. (A voter sent me an even WORSE version of this, performed by actress Julie London, who at one time—and don't tell me this is mere coincidence—was married to Jack Webb.)

Coming in a strong third is "(You're) Having My Baby" by Paul Anka. This song is deeply hated. As one voter put it: "It has no redeeming value whatsoever—except my friend Brian yelled out during the birth scene in the sequel to *The Fly* in full song, 'Having my maggot!' "

Honorable mention goes to Bobby Goldsboro, who got many votes for various songs, especially "Honey." One voter wrote: "Why does everybody hate Bobby Goldsboro's 'Honey'? I hate it too, but I want to know WHY."

Why? Consider this verse: "She wrecked the car and she was sad; And so afraid that I'd be mad, but what the heck; Tho' I pretended hard to be; Guess you could say she saw through me; And hugged my neck."

As one reader observed: "Bobby never caught on that he could have bored a hole in himself and let the sap out."

A recent song that has aroused great hostility is "Achy Breaky Heart," by Billy Ray Cyrus. According to voter Mark Freeman, the song sounds like this: "You can tell my lips, or you can tell my hips, that you're going to dump me if you can; But don't tell my liver, it never would forgive her, it might blow up and circumcise this man!"

Many voters feel a special Lifetime Bad Achievement Award should go to Mac Davis, who wrote "In the Ghetto," "Watching Scotty Grow," AND "Baby Don't Get Hooked on Me," which contains one of the worst lines in musical history: "You're a hot-blooded woman, child; And it's warm where you're touching me." That might be as bad as the part in "Careless Whisper" where George Michael sings: "I'm never gonna dance again; Guilty feet have got no rhythm."

Speaking of bad lyrics, many voters also cited Paul Mc-Cartney, who, ever since his body was taken over by a pod person, has been writing things like: "Someone's knockin' at the door; Somebody's ringin' the bell; (repeat); Do me a favor, open the door, and let him in."

There were strong votes for various tragedy songs, especially "Teen Angel" ("I'll never kiss your lips again; They buried you today") and "Timothy," a song about—really—three trapped miners, two of whom wind up eating the third.

Other tremendously unpopular songs, for their lyrics or overall badness, are: "Muskrat Love," "Sugar Sugar," "I'm Too Sexy," "Surfin' Bird," "I've Never Been to Me," "In-a-Gadda-Da-Vida," "Afternoon Delight," "Feelings," "You Light Up My Life," and "In the Year 2525" (*violent* hatred for this song).

In closing, let me say that you voters have performed a major public service, and that just because your song didn't make the list, that doesn't mean it isn't awful (unless you were one of the badly misguided people who voted for "The Tupperware Song"). Let me also say that I am very relieved to learn that there are people besides me who hate "Stairway to Heaven." Thank you.

P.S. Also "I Shot the Sheriff."

This is the last section; like the first one, it's mostly family stuff. It includes a column I wrote when my son got hit by a car, which was very scary; and one about his reaching adolescence, which veteran parents have assured me will be even scarier. There is also some important advice in here for young people, who represent our nation's Hope for the Future. I myself plan to be dead.

THE OLD-TIMERS GAME

My son got his ear pierced. He's 12. For 12 years I worked hard to prevent him from developing unnatural bodily holes, then he went out and got one on purpose. At a *shopping mall*. It turns out that minors can have their earlobes assaulted with sharp implements by shopping-mall-booth personnel who, for all we know, have received no more formal medical training than is given to burrito folders at Taco Bell. And the failed Clinton administration is doing *nothing*.

You're probably saying: "Don't blame the government! As a parent, YOU must take responsibility! You and your wife, Beth, should sit your son down and give him a stern reprimand."

Listen, that's a great idea, except for one teensy little problem, which is that BETH IS THE PERSON WHO DROVE HIM TO THE PIERCING PLACE. This is the same woman who, when Rob was 6, allowed him to get a "punk" style haircut that transformed him in just a few minutes from Christopher Robin into Bart Simpson; the same woman who indulges his taste for clothes that appear to have been dyed in radioactive Kool-Aid.

No, Beth is not on my side in the ongoing battle I have waged with my son to keep him normal, defined as "like me, but with less nose hair."

Now you're probably saying: "Who are YOU to be complaining? When you were young, didn't YOU feel you had the right to do things that your parents disapproved of?" Perhaps you are referring to the time in ninth grade when Phil Grant, Tom Parker, and I decided that pipe-smoking was cool, so we got hold of some pipes and stood around spewing smoke, thinking we looked like urbane sophisticates, when in fact we looked like the Junior Fred Mac-Murray Dork Patrol. I will admit that when my parents found out about this (following a minor desk fire in my room) and told me to stop, I went into a week-long door-slamming snit, as though the right of ninth-graders to smoke pipes was explicitly stated in the U.S. Constitution.

But we cannot compare these two situations. In the case of my pipe-smoking, my parents were clearly overreacting, because the worst that could have happened was that I would have burned the house down and got cancer. Whereas I have a very good reason to object to Rob's earlobe hole: It makes me feel old. Rob wears a little jeweled ear stud, and it's constantly winking at me and saying: "Hey there, old-timer! YOU'D never wear an ear stud! And neither would Grandpa Walton!"

I am also being rapidly aged by Rob's choice of radio stations. The one he now prefers is operated by one of the most dangerous and irresponsible forces on Earth, college students. I was concerned about what they might be playing, so I tuned it in on my car radio. The first song I heard didn't sound so bad, and I said to myself: "Hey! Perhaps I am still fairly hip after all!" And then the deejay came on and said, apologetically: "I realize that song was *mainstream.*" He said "mainstream" the way you would say "composed by Phoenicians." Then he played a song entitled—I am not making this up—"Detachable Penis."

Yes, college students are in on the plot with my son to make me feel old. Not long ago I was sitting on a beach near a group of male college students who were talking about a bungee-jumping excursion they had taken. They were bragging about the fact that they had leaped off the tower in the *only* cool way, which is headfirst and backward. They spoke with great contempt about a group of fathers—that's the term they used, "fathers," making it sound as though it means "people even older than Phoenicians''—who had jumped off feet-first, which the college students considered to be pathetic.

This made me feel *extremely* old, because I personally would not bungee-jump off the *Oxford English Dictionary*. My son, on the other hand, would unhesitatingly bungee-jump off the Concorde. And he's only *12*. Who KNOWS how old he'll make me feel by the time he's 14. What if he wants a *nose ring?* I won't allow it! I'm going to put my foot down! I'm going to take charge!

I'm going to steal Beth's car keys.

BREAKING THE ICE

As a mature adult, I feel an obligation to help the younger generation, just as the mother fish guards her unhatched eggs, keeping her lonely vigil day after day, never leaving her post, not even to go to the bathroom, until her tiny babies emerge and she is able, at last, to eat them. "She may be your mom, but she's still a fish" is a wisdom nugget that I would pass along to any fish eggs reading this column.

But today I want to talk about dating. This subject was raised in a letter to me from a young person named Eric Knott, who writes:

> I have got a big problem. There's this girl in my English class who is *really* good-looking. However, I don't think she knows I exist. I want to ask her out, but I'm afraid she will say no, and I will be the freak of the week. What should I do?

Eric, you have sent your question to the right mature adult, because as a young person I spent a lot of time thinking about this very problem. Starting in about eighth grade, my time was divided as follows:

Academic Pursuits: 2 percent.
Zits: 16 percent.
Trying to Figure Out How to Ask Girls Out: 82 percent.

The most sensible way to ask a girl out is to walk directly up to her on foot and say, "So, you want to go out? Or what?" I never did this. I knew, as Eric Knott knows, that there was always the possibility that the girl would say no, thereby leaving me with no viable option but to leave Harold C. Crittenden Junior High School forever and go into the woods and become a bark-eating hermit whose only companions would be the gentle and understanding woodland creatures.

"Hey, ZITFACE!" the woodland creatures would shriek in cute little Chip 'n' Dale voices while raining acorns down upon my head. "You wanna DATE? HAHAHAHA-HAHA."

So the first rule of dating is: Never risk direct contact with the girl in question. Your role model should be the nuclear submarine, gliding silently beneath the ocean surface, tracking an enemy target that does not even begin to suspect that the submarine would like to date it. I spent the vast majority of 1960 keeping a girl named Judy under surveillance, maintaining a minimum distance of 50 lockers to avoid the danger that I might somehow get into a conversation with her, which could have led to disaster:

JUDY: Hi.

ME: Hi.

JUDY: Just in case you have ever thought about having a date with me, the answer is no.

WOODLAND CREATURES: HAHAHAHAHAHA.

The only problem with the nuclear-submarine technique is that it's difficult to get a date with a girl who has never, technically, been asked. This is why you need Phil Grant. Phil was a friend of mine who had the ability to talk to girls. It was a mysterious superhuman power he had, comparable to X-ray vision. So, after several thousand hours of intense discussion and planning with me, Phil approached a girl he knew named Nancy, who approached a girl named Sandy, who was a direct personal friend of Judy's and who passed the word back to Phil via Nancy that Judy would be willing to go on a date with me. This procedure protected me from direct humiliation, similar to the way President Reagan was protected from direct involvement in the Iran-contra scandal by a complex White House chain of command that at one point, investigators now believe, included his horse.

203

Thus it was that, finally, Judy and I went on an actual date, to see a movie in White Plains, New York. If I were to sum up the romantic ambience of this date in four words, those words would be: "My mother was driving." This made for an extremely quiet drive, because my mother, realizing that her presence was hideously embarrassing, had to pretend she wasn't there. If it had been legal, I think she would have got out and sprinted alongside the car, steering through the window. Judy and I, sitting in the backseat about 75 feet apart, were also silent, unable to communicate without the assistance of Phil, Nancy, and Sandy.

After what seemed like several years we got to the movie theater, where my mother went off to sit in the Parents and Lepers Section. The movie was called *North to Alaska,* but I can tell you nothing else about it because I spent the whole time wondering whether it would be necessary to amputate my right arm, which was not getting any blood flow as a result of being perched for two hours like a petrified snake on the back of Judy's seat exactly one molecule away from physical contact.

So it was definitely a fun first date, featuring all the relaxed spontaneity of a real-estate closing, and in later years I did regain some feeling in my arm. My point, Eric Knott, is that the key to successful dating is *self-confidence.* I bet that good-looking girl in your English class would LOVE to go out with you. But YOU have to make the first move. So just do it! Pick up that phone! Call Phil Grant.

CONSUMERS FROM MARS

Recently I was watching TV, and a commercial came on, and the announcer, in a tone of voice usually reserved for major developments in the Persian Gulf, said: "Now consumers can ask Angela Lansbury their questions about Bufferin!"

As a normal human, your natural reaction to this announcement is: "Huh?" Meaning: "What does Angela Lansbury have to do with Bufferin?" But this commercial featured several consumers who had apparently been stopped at random on the street, and *every one of them had a question for Angela Lansbury about Bufferin*. Basically what they asked was, "Miss Lansbury, is Bufferin a good product that I should purchase, or what?" These consumers seemed very earnest. It was as if they had been going around for months wringing their hands and saying, "I have a question about Bufferin! If only I could ask Angela Lansbury!"

What we are seeing here is yet another example of a worsening problem that has been swept under the rug for too long in this nation: the invasion of Consumers from

Consumers from Mars

THIS SEEMS LIKE AN AWFULLY BAD DEAL FOR THE HUGE, FACELESS MULTINATIONAL CONGLOMERATE THAT MAKES THIS PRODUCT... PERHAPS THEY COULD PUT LESS IN THE BOX AND CHARGE MORE...

Mars. They *look* like humans, but they don't *act* like humans, and they are taking over. Don't laugh. We know that Mars can support life. We know this because Vice President for Now Dan Quayle, who is the administration's No. 1 Man in the space program, once made the following famous statement, which I am not making up:

"Mars is essentially in the same orbit . . . somewhat the same distance from the Sun, which is very important. We have seen pictures where there are canals, we believe, and water. If there is water, that means there is oxygen. If oxygen, that means we can breathe."

You cannot argue with that kind of logic. You can only carry it to its logical conclusion, which is that if there are canals, that means there are boats, and if there are boats, that means there are consumers, and apparently they are invading the Earth and getting on TV commercials.

I saw another commercial recently wherein a middle-age man gets off an airplane and is greeted by his wife, who says something like: "What did you bring back from your trip?" And the man replies: "Diarrhea." Yes. He probably hasn't seen his wife in a week, and the first thing out of his mouth, so to speak, is "Diarrhea." Is this the behavior of a regular (ha ha!) human? Of course not. This is clearly another invading consumer from Mars, just like the ones that are always striding into drugstores and announcing at the top of their lungs that they have hemorrhoids.

The worst thing is that, as Martian consumers take over, they're starting to influence the way businesses think. I received chilling evidence of this recently from alert reader Rick Johansen, who sent me an Associated Press article by David Kalish about food manufacturers who are putting less food into packages, but not reducing prices. One example was Knorr brand leek soup and recipe mix: The old box contained four eight-ounce servings, but the new box, which is slightly larger, contains only *three* eight-ounce servings. The story quotes a spokesperson for the manufacturer, CPC International, as saying that this change was made because—pay close attention here—there were "a lot of complaints from American consumers that we were giving them too much in the box."

Sure! We believe that! We believe that all over America, consumers were sitting around their dinner tables, saying, "You know Ralph, I am sick and tired of getting so much soup in a box. I'm going to write in and demand that they put less in without lowering the price."

"Good idea!" Ralph would answer, pounding his fist on

the table. "And then let's tell Angela Lansbury about our hemorrhoids!"

No, those were not American consumers who complained to CPC International; those were Martians. Also, most product instructions are now written for Martians. Alert reader Mark Lindsay sent me the instructions for the Sunbeam Dental Water Jet; under the heading IMPORTANT SAFEGUARDS is the statement—I am still not making this up—"Never use while sleeping." Don't try to tell me that's for Earthlings.

And how about all those manufacturers' coupons featuring Exciting Offers wherein it turns out, when you read the fine print, that you have to send in the coupon PLUS proof of purchase PLUS your complete dental records by registered mail to Greenland and allow at least 18 months for them to send you ANOTHER coupon that will entitle you to 29 cents off your next purchase of a product you don't really want? Do you think anybody besides extraterrestrials ever actually *does* that?

I have here a package sent in by alert reader Roger Lyons, who purchased a Revlon Pedi-Care Toe Nail Clip device for $2.19 at a Giant Supermarket in Washington, D.C. On the package is Revlon's Full Lifetime Guarantee, which states that if you find any defects, you should follow this procedure:

Wrap securely in a box or mailing tube . . . Mail insured and POSTAGE PAID . . . Notify us within six months if implement is not returned . . . GUARANTEE IS NOT APPLICABLE if implement has been serviced by other than Revlon, has been abused or allowed to rust. Keep lightly oiled in a dry place to avoid rusting . . .

And so on. Who would DO this? Who would ever think of saving the package so he or she would know HOW to do this? Only Martians! Face it, human consumers: They have taken over. It's too late to do anything about it. Your best bet is to stay calm, remain indoors, maybe oil your toenail clippers. Me, I have to set up the landing lights on my lawn. Zorkon is bringing in a new group tonight.

SAY UNCLE

Summer vacation is almost over, so today Uncle Dave has a special back-to-school "pep talk" for you young people, starting with these heartfelt words of encouragement: HA HA HA YOU HAVE TO GO BACK TO SCHOOL AND UNCLE DAVE DOESN'T NEENER NEENER NEENER.

Seriously, young people, I have some important back-to-school advice for you, and I can boil it down to four simple words: "Study Your Mathematics."

I say this in light of a recent alarming Associated Press story stating that three out of every four high-school students—nearly 50 percent—leave school without an adequate understanding of mathematics. Frankly, I am not surprised. "How," I am constantly asking myself, "can we expect today's young people to understand mathematics when so many of them *can't even point their baseball caps in the right direction?*"

I am constantly seeing young people with the bills of their baseball caps pointing *backward*. This makes no sense, young people! If you examine your cap closely, you will note that it has a piece sticking out the front called a "bill." The purpose of the bill is to keep sun off your face, which, unless your parents did a great many drugs in the '60s (Ask them about it!), is located on the FRONT of your head. Wearing your cap backward is like wearing sunglasses on the back of your head, or wearing a hearing aid in your nose. (Perhaps you young people are doing this also. Uncle Dave doesn't want to know.)

So to summarize what we've learned: "FRONT of cap goes on FRONT of head." Got it, young people? Let's all strive to do better in the coming school year!

But also we need to think about getting these math scores up. A shocking number of you young people are

unable to solve even basic math problems, such as the following:

A customer walks into a fast-food restaurant, orders two hamburgers costing $2 apiece, then hands you a $5 bill. How much change should you give him?

a. $2
b. $3
c. None, because the question doesn't say you WORK there. You could just take the money and run away.

The correct answer, of course, is that you should give the customer:

d. Whatever the computerized cash register says, even if it's $154,789.62.

You young people must learn to handle basic mathematical concepts such as this if you hope to ever become a smug and complacent older person such as myself. I was fortunate enough to receive an excellent mathematical foundation as a member of the Class of 196.5 Billion Years Ago at Pleasantville High School, where I studied math under Mr. Solin, who, in my senior year, attempted to teach us calculus (from the ancient Greek words *calc,* meaning "the study of," and *ulus,* meaning "something that only Mr. Solin could understand").

Mr. Solin was an excellent teacher, and although the subject matter was dry, he was able to keep the class's attention riveted on him from the moment the bell rang until the moment, several minutes later, when a large girls' gym class walked past the classroom windows, every single day, causing the heads of us male students to rotate 90 mathematical degrees in unison, like elves in a motorized Christmas yard display. But during those brief periods when we were facing Mr. Solin, we received a solid foundation in mathematics, learning many important mathematical concepts that we still use in our professional lives as employees of top U.S. corporations. A good example is the mathematical concept of "9," which we use almost daily to obtain an outside line on our corporate telephones so that we can order Chinese food, place bets, call 1-900-BOSOMS, and perform all of the other vital employee functions that make our economy what it is today.

You young people deserve to have the same advantages, which is why I was so pleased to note in the Associated Press story that some university professors have received a $6 million federal grant to develop new ways to teach math to high-school students. The professors know this will be a challenge. One of them is quoted as saying: "There is a mentality in this country that mathematics is something a few nerds out there do and if you don't understand mathematics, it's OK—you don't need it."

This is a bad mentality, young people. There's nothing "nerdy" about mathematics. Contrary to their image as a bunch of out-of-it huge-butted Far Side–professor dweebs who spend all day staring at incomprehensible symbols on a blackboard while piles of dandruff form around their ankles, today's top mathematicians are in fact a group of exciting, dynamic, and glamorous individuals who are working to solve some of the most fascinating and challenging problems facing the human race today ("Let's see, at $2.98 apiece, with a $6 million federal grant, we could buy . . . WHOA! That's 2,013,422.82 POCKET PROTECTORS!").

So come on, young people! Get in on the action! Work hard in math this year, and remember this: If some muscle-bound Neanderthal bullies corner you in the bathroom and call you a "nerd," you just look them straight in the eye and say, "Oh YEAH? Why don't you big jerks . . . LET GO! HEY! DON'T PUT MY HEAD IN THE TOILET! HEY!" And tell them that goes double for your Uncle Dave.

PUNCTUATION 'R EASY

It's time for another edition of "Ask Mister Language Person," the column that answers your questions about grammar, vocabulary, and those little whaddyacallem marks.

Q. What are the rules regarding capital letters?

A. Capital letters are used in three grammatical situations:

1. At the beginning of proper or formal nouns.

EXAMPLES: Capitalize "Queen," "Tea Party," and "Rental Tuxedo." Do NOT capitalize "dude," "cha-cha," or "boogerhead."

2. To indicate a situation of great military importance.

EXAMPLE: "Get on the TELSAT and tell STAFCON that COMWIMP wants some BBQ ASAP."

3. To indicate that the subject of the sentence has been bitten by a badger.

EXAMPLE: "I'll just stick my hand in here and OUCH!"

Q. Is there any difference between "happen" and "transpire"?

215

A. Grammatically, "happen" is a collaborating inductive that should be used in predatory conjunctions such as: "Me and Norm here would like to buy you two happening mommas a drink." Whereas "transpire" is a suppository verb that should always be used to indicate that an event of some kind has transpired.

WRONG: "Lester got one of them electric worm stunners."

RIGHT: "What transpired was, Lester got one of them electric worm stunners."

Q. Do you take questions from attorneys?

A. Yes. That will be $475.

Q. No, seriously, I'm an attorney, and I want to know which is correct:

"With regards to the aforementioned" blah blah blah.
Or:
"With regards to the aforementioned" yak yak yak.

A. That will be $850.

Q. Please explain the expression: "This does not bode well."

A. It means that something is not boding the way it should. It could be boding better.

Q. Did an alert reader named Linda Bevard send you an article from the December 19, 1990, *Denver Post* concerning a Dr. Stanley Biber, who was elected commissioner in Las Animas County, and who is identified in the article as "the world's leading sex-change surgeon"?

A. Yes.

Q. And what did Dr. Biber say when he was elected?
A. He said, quote: "We pulled it off."

Q. Please explain the correct usage of "exact same."

A. "Exact same" is a corpuscular phrase that should be used only when something is exactly the same as something. It is the opposite (or "antibody") of "a whole nother."

EXAMPLE: "This is the exact same restaurant where Alma found weevils in her pie. They gave her a whole nother slice."

Q. I am going to deliver the eulogy at a funeral, and I wish to know whether it is correct to say: "Before he died, LaMont was an active person." Or: "LaMont was an active person before he died."

A. The American Funeral Industry Council advises us that the preferred term is "bought the farm."

Q. Where should punctuation go?
A. It depends on the content.

EXAMPLE: Hi Mr Johnson exclaimed Bob Where do you want me to put these punctuation marks Oh just stick them there at the end of the following sentence answered Mr Johnson OK said Bob ".!".".?"".,.."..".!".

The exception to this rule is teenagers, who should place a question mark after every few words to make sure people are still listening.

EXAMPLE: "So there's this kid at school? Named Derrick? And he's like kind of weird? Like he has a picture of Newt Gingrich carved in his hair? So one day he had to blow his nose? Like really bad? But he didn't have a tissue? So he was like sitting next to Tracy Steakle? And she had this sweater? By like Ralph Lauren? So Derrick takes the sleeve? And he like . . ."

PROFESSIONAL WRITING TIP: In writing a novel or play, use "foreshadowing" to subtly hint at the outcome of the plot.

WRONG: "O Romeo, Romeo, wherefore art thou Romeo?"

RIGHT: "O Romeo, Romeo! I wonder if we're both going to stab ourselves to death at the end of this plot?"

YOU'VE GOTTA
BE KIDDING

TODAY'S SCARY TOPIC FOR PARENTS IS: What Your Children Do When You're Not Home.

I have here a letter from Buffalo, New York, from working mom Judy Price, concerning her 14-year-old son, David, "who should certainly know better, because the school keeps telling me he is a genius, but I have not seen signs of this in our normal, everyday life."

Judy states that one day when she came home from work, David met her outside and said: "Hi, Mom. Are you going in?"

(This is a bad sign, parents.)

Judy says she considered replying, "No, I thought I'd just stay here in the car all night and pull away for work in the morning."

That actually would have been a wise idea. Instead, she went inside, where she found a large black circle burned into the middle of her kitchen counter.

"DAVID," she screamed. "WHAT WERE YOU COOKING?"

The soft, timid reply came back: "A baseball."

"A *baseball*," Judy writes. "Of *course*. What else could it be? How could I forget to tell my children never to cook a baseball? It's my fault, really."

It turns out that according to David's best friend's cousin—and if you can't believe HIM, who CAN you believe?—you can hit a baseball three times as far if you really heat it up first. So David did this, and naturally he put the red-hot pan down directly onto the countertop, probably because there was no rare antique furniture available.

For the record: David claims that the heated baseball did, in fact, go farther. But this does NOT mean that you young readers should try this foolish and dangerous experiment at home. Use a friend's home.

No, seriously, you young people should never heat a baseball without proper adult supervision, just as you should never—and I say this from personal experience—attempt to make a rumba box.

A rumba box is an obscure musical instrument that consists of a wooden box with metal strips attached to it in such a way that when you plunk them, the box resonates with a pleasant rhythmic sound. The only time I ever saw a rumba box was in 1964, when a friend of my parents named Walter Karl played one at a gathering at our house, and it sounded great. Mr. Karl explained that the metal strips were actually pieces of the spring from an old-fashioned wind-up phonograph. This gave my best friend, Lanny Watts, an idea.

Lanny was always having ideas. For example, one day he got tired of walking to the end of his driveway to get the mail, so he had the idea of hanging the mailbox from a rope-and-pulley system strung up the driveway to his porch, where he hooked it up to a washing-machine motor. When the mailman came, Lanny simply plugged in the motor, and *whoosh,* the mailbox fell down. The amount of time Lanny spent unsuccessfully trying to get this labor-saving device to work was equivalent to approximately 5,000 trips to get the actual mail, but that is the price of convenience.

So anyway, when Lanny heard Mr. Karl explain the rumba box, he realized two things:

1. His parents had an old-fashioned wind-up phonograph they hardly ever used.
2. They both worked out of the home.

So Lanny and I decided to make our own rumba box. Our plan, as I recall it, was to take the phonograph apart, snip off a bit of the spring, then put the phonograph back together, and nobody would be the wiser. This plan worked perfectly until we removed the metal box that held the phonograph spring; this box turned out to be very hard to open.

"Why would they make it so *strong?*" we asked ourselves.

Finally, recalling the lessons we had learned about mechanical advantage in high-school physics class, we decided to hit the box with a sledge hammer.

Do you remember the climactic scene in the movie *Raiders of the Lost Ark,* when the Nazis open up the Ark of the Covenant and out surges a terrifying horde of evil fury and the Nazis' heads melt like chocolate bunnies in a microwave? Well, that's similar to what happened when Lanny sledge-hammered the spring box. It turns out that the reason the box is so strong is that there is a really powerful, tightly wound, extremely irritable spring in there, and when you let it out, it just goes *berserk,* writhing and snarling and thrashing violently all over the room, seeking to gain revenge on all the people who have cranked it over the years.

Lanny and I fled the room until the spring calmed down. When we returned, we found phonograph parts spread all over the room, mixed in with approximately 2.4 miles of spring. We realized we'd have to modify our Project Goal slightly, from making a rumba box to being in an entirely new continent when Lanny's mom got home.

Actually, Mrs. Watts went fairly easy on us, just as Judy Price seems to have been good-humored about her son's heating the baseball. Moms are usually pretty good that way.

But sometimes I wonder. You know how guys are always complaining that they used to have a baseball-card collection that would be worth a fortune today if they still had it, but their moms threw it out? And the guys always say, "Mom just didn't know any better."

Well, I wonder if the moms knew *exactly* what they were doing.

Getting even.

SEXUAL INTERCOURSE

Today's Topic for Guys is: Communicating with Women.

If there's one thing that women find unsatisfactory about guys—and I base this conclusion on an extensive scientific study of the pile of *Cosmopolitan* magazines where I get my hair cut—it is that guys do not communicate enough.

This problem has arisen in my own personal relationship with my wife, Beth. I'll be reading the newspaper and the phone will ring; I'll answer it, listen for 10 minutes, hang up, and resume reading. Finally Beth will say: "Who was that?"

And I'll say, "Phil Wonkerman's mom."

Phil is an old friend we haven't heard from in 17 years. And Beth will say, "Well?"

And I'll say, "Well what?"

And Beth will say, "What did she SAY?"

And I'll say, "She said Phil is fine," making it clear by my tone of voice that, although I do not wish to be rude, I AM trying to read the newspaper here, and I happen to be right in the middle of an important panel of "Calvin and Hobbes."

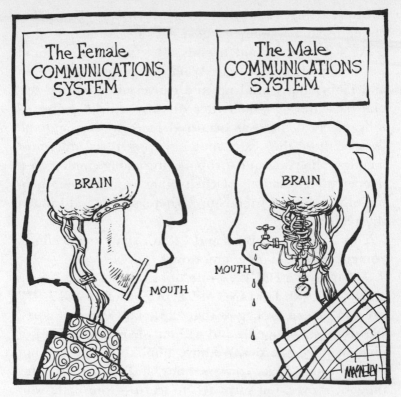

But Beth, ignoring this, will say, "That's ALL she said?"
And she will not let up. She will continue to ask district
attorney–style questions, forcing me to recount the conversation until she's satisfied that she has the entire story,
which is that Phil just got out of prison after serving a
sentence for a murder he committed when he became a
drug addict because of the guilt he felt when his wife died
in a freak submarine accident while Phil was having an
affair with a nun, but now he's all straightened out and
has a good job as a trapeze artist and is almost through
with the surgical part of his sex change and just became
happily engaged to marry a prominent member of New
Kids on the Block, so in other words he is fine, which is

EXACTLY what I told Beth in the first place, but is that enough? No. She wants to hear *every single detail*.

We have some good friends, Buzz and Libby, whom we see about twice a year. When we get together, Beth and Libby always wind up in a conversation, lasting several days, during which they discuss virtually every significant event that has occurred in their lives and the lives of those they care about, sharing their innermost feelings, analyzing and probing, inevitably coming to a deeper understanding of each other, and a strengthening of a cherished friendship. Whereas Buzz and I watch the playoffs.

This is not to say Buzz and I don't share our feelings. Sometimes we get quite emotional.

"That's not a FOUL??" one of us will say.

Or: "YOU'RE TELLING ME THAT'S NOT A *FOUL*???"

I don't mean to suggest that all we talk about is sports. We also discuss, openly and without shame, what kind of pizza we need to order. We have a fine time together, but we don't have heavy conversations, and sometimes, after the visit is over, I'm surprised to learn—from Beth, who learned it from Libby—that there has recently been some new wrinkle in Buzz's life, such as that he now has an artificial leg.

(For the record, Buzz does NOT have an artificial leg. At least he didn't mention anything about it to me.)

I have another good friend, Gene, who's going through major developments in his life. Our families recently spent a weekend together, during which Gene and I talked a lot and enjoyed each other's company immensely. In that entire time, the most intimate personal statement he made to me is that he has reached Level 24 of a video game called Arkanoid. He has even seen the Evil Presence, although he refused to tell me what it looks like. We're very close, but there is a limit.

I know what some of you are saying. You're saying my friends and I are Neanderthals, and a lot of guys are different. This is true. A lot of guys don't use words at *all*. They communicate entirely by nonverbal methods, such as sharing bait.

But my point, guys, is that you must communicate on a deeper level with a woman, particularly if you are married to her. Open up. Don't assume that she knows what you're thinking. This will be difficult for guys at first, so it would help if you women would try to "read between the lines" in determining what the guy is trying to communicate:

GUY STATEMENT: "Do we have any peanut butter?"

INNER GUY MEANING: "I hate my job."

GUY STATEMENT: "Is this all we have? Crunchy?"

INNER GUY MEANING: "I'm not sure I want to stay married."

If both genders work together, you can have a happier, healthier relationship, but the responsibility rests with you guys, who must sincerely . . . Hey, guys, I'm TALKING to you here. Put down the sports section, OK? HEY! GUYS!

NERDS "Я" US

COMMENCEMENT ADDRESS TO THE HIGH-SCHOOL GRADUATING CLASS OF 1992: As I look out over your shining faces, I am reminded of the Bartlett's familiar quotation by the great Greek philosopher Socrates, who said, "Eventually your skin will clear up and your faces won't shine so much."

As is so often the case with great philosophers, he was lying. Your skin is a lifelong enemy, young people. It has millions of hardy zit cells that will continue to function perfectly, long after the rest of your organs have become aged and decrepit. Remember Ronald Reagan? No? Well, he used to be the president, off and on, and in 1985, after undergoing a medical procedure on his nose, he met with the press and made the following two statements, which I swear to you young people that I am not making up:

1. "It is true I had—well, I guess for want of a better word—a pimple on my nose."
2. "I violated all the rules. I picked at it and I squoze it and so forth and messed myself up a little."

228

And President Reagan was no spring chicken at the time. I believe that, at one point in his acting career, he actually was in a movie with Socrates. The point I am making, young people, is that your skin will *never* "clear up." People have been known to break out with embarrassing blemishes at their own funerals.

But postmortem acne is not what you young people should be thinking about today as you prepare to go out into the world, leaving behind the hallowed halls of your school, but not before sticking wads of gum on virtually every hallowed surface. Perhaps you think you have gotten away with this. You may be interested to learn that, thanks to a Used Gum Tracing procedure developed by the FBI,

school authorities can now analyze the DNA in the dried-spit molecules and, by cross-referencing with your Permanent Record, determine *exactly who was chewing every single wad*. This means that someday in the future—perhaps at your wedding—burly officers of the Gum Police will come barging in and arrest you and take you off to harsh prisons where you will be forced to eat food prepared by *the same people who ran your high-school cafeteria.*

Yes, young people, modern technology promises an exciting future. But you must also learn from the wisdom of your elders, and if there is one piece of advice that I would offer you, it is this: Burn your yearbook right now. Because otherwise, years from now, feeling nostalgic, you'll open it up to your photo, and this alien GEEK will be staring out at you, and your children will beg you to tell them that they're adopted.

It is a known science fact that, no matter how good your yearbook photo looks now, after 15 years of being pressed up against somebody else's face in the dark and mysterious yearbook environment, it will transmutate itself into a humiliating picture of a total goober. This is true of everybody. If, in early 1991, the U.S. government had quietly contacted Saddam Hussein and threatened to publish his yearbook photo in the *New York Times,* he would have dropped Kuwait like a 250-pound maggot.

Yes, young people, old yearbook photos can be a powerful force for good. Yet the horrifying truth is that sometimes newspapers publish the yearbook photos of *totally innocent people.* Yes! In America! I know what I'm talking about, young people, because it happened to me. The March 1992 issue of *Panther Tracks,* the newspaper of my alma mater, Pleasantville (New York) High School, has an article about me, and although I definitely remember looking normal in high school, there's a photograph of this solemn little Junior Certified Public Accountant wearing glasses styled by Mister Bob's House of Soviet Eyewear.

People I hadn't heard from in years mailed me this picture, along with heartwarming and thoughtful notes. "Dave!" they'd say. "I forgot what a DWEEB you were!" Or: "Who styled your hair? Bigfoot?"

This is unfair, Class of '92. Let me assure you that I was very "hip" in high school. I distinctly remember an incident in 1964, when Lanny Watts and I got a stern lecture from the assistant principal, Mr. Sabella, because we showed up at a school dance with our sport-jacket collars turned under, so the jackets looked like they didn't HAVE collars, because this was the style worn by the Dave Clark Five. Remember the Dave Clark Five, young people? No? Sure you do! You must! They had that big hit with the drum part that went: WHOMPA WHOMPA WHOMPA

Wasn't that a great song, young people? Hey, are you *laughing* at me? STOP LAUGHING AT ME, YOU LITTLE ZITFACES!

Thank you.

UNEASY RIDER

It's 6 P.M., and we're waiting for our 12-year-old son, Rob, to return from a quick bike ride. We're going to go out to dinner to celebrate the fact that, for the 1,000th consecutive night, we have figured out an excuse to not cook at home.

We're locking up the house when a young man comes to the door and asks if we have a son.

"There's been an accident," he says.

"Is it bad?" Beth asks.

"There's blood everywhere," he says.

Sometimes I wonder if parenthood is such a good idea. Sometimes I envy fish and frogs and lobsters and other animals that just emit their young in egg form, then swim or hop or lobster-scoot away from the scene, free of responsibility, immune from anguish. I can remember when there was nobody in my world as important to me as me. Oh, I loved other people—my wife, my family, my friends—and I would have been distraught if something bad happened to them. But I knew I'd still be here. And that was the really important thing.

NERDY BICYCLE HELMET:

MUCH NERDIER HOSPITAL HELMET:

Rob changed that. Right at birth. When he came out, looking like a cranky old prune, he didn't cry. Beth, instantly a mom, kept saying, through her haze of labor pain, "Why isn't he crying? Why isn't he crying?" The nurse said sometimes they don't cry, but I could see that the doctor thought something was wrong, because he was trying to do something with Rob's mouth, and he was having trouble. He whispered something to the nurse and took Rob away, and the nurse kept saying this was routine, but we knew it wasn't. I stood there, wearing my goofy hospital outfit, holding Beth's hand, trying to cope with two staggering thoughts: First, I had a child—*I had a child*—and second, *maybe my child was in trouble.*

That was the most sickeningly vulnerable feeling I'd ever felt.

And I didn't even know Rob yet.

It turned out he was OK—just a little blockage. The doctor gave him back to us, and we quickly became traditional first-time parents, wrapped in a woozy cocoon of joy and exhaustion, taking a genuine intellectual interest in poop, marveling at the thrill we felt, the *connection*, when our son's tiny hand squeezed our fingers.

But the feeling of vulnerability didn't go away. It only got worse, always lurking inside, forcing me to accept that I wasn't in control anymore, not when I knew my universe could be trashed at any moment because of unpredictable, uncontrollable developments on this newborn comet, zooming through. When he was happy, I was happier than I'd ever been; but when he was in trouble . . . I can remember every detail of the time when, at 10 months, he got a bad fever, 106 degrees, his tiny body burning, and I carried him into the hospital, thinking *I can't take this, please, let me be able to stop this, please, give me this fever, take it out of this little boy and put it in me, please. . . .*

But you can't do that. You can't make it happen to you. You have to watch it happen to your child, and it never gets any easier, does it?

Now Beth and I are in the car, and I'm driving too fast, but I have to; I have to see what I don't want to see. Up ahead some people are gathered on the side of the road, and a woman is kneeling—she has blood on her dress, a lot of blood—and lying in front of her, on his back, his face covered with blood is . . .

"Oh God," says Beth. "Oh God."

This is where it ends, for some parents. Right here, on the roadside. My heart breaks for these parents. I don't know that I could survive it.

Now I'm opening the door, stumbling out of the car toward Rob. He's moving his right hand. *He's waving at me.* He's giving me a weak, bloody smile, trying to reassure me.

"It's my fault," he's saying. "I'm sorry. It's my fault."

"It's OK!" I'm saying. "It's OK!"

Please let it be OK.

"I'm sorry," the bloody-dress woman is saying. "I'm so sorry." She was driving the car that collided with Rob. He went through the windshield, then was thrown back out onto the road, 40 feet, according to the ambulance guys.

"This is my worst nightmare," the woman is saying.

"I'm sorry," Rob is saying.

"It's OK!" I'm saying. "You're going to be OK!"

Please.

He was OK. A broken leg, some skin scraped off, a lot of stitches, but nothing that won't heal. He'll be getting out of his cast in a couple of months, getting on with his ever-busier life, his friends, his school, his stuff; he'll be growing bigger, moving faster, this bright comet-boy who streaked into my universe 12 years ago and is already starting to arc his way back out, farther from me, from my control, from my sight.

But that little hand will never let go of my finger.

I'm sorry. This was supposed to be a hilarious column about how Beth and I were getting ready to go out for a nice dinner at 6 P.M. and wound up eating lukewarm cheeseburgers at 11 P.M. on a table in the Miami Children's Hospital emergency room; and how Rob, after politely thanking a very nice nurse for helping him sit up, threw up on her; and other comical events. But this is how the column turned out. Next week I promise to return to Booger Journalism.

In closing, here's a Public Service Message for you young readers from Rob Barry, who won't be walking for a while but can still operate a keyboard:

I know that bike helmets look really nerdy, and that was my argument. But I don't think I'll ever say that again. Make SURE you wear your helmets. And WATCH OUT FOR CARS.

DAVE'S REAL WORLD

The reason I agreed to be in an episode of a TV situation comedy was that the role was perfect for me. You want to choose your roles carefully, as an actor. You want to look for roles in which you can display the range, the depth, the infinitely subtle nuances of your acting talent.

"It's just one word," the director said. "You say 'Howdy.'"

"I'll do it," I said. A role like that comes along once in a lifetime.

The TV show—which might even still be on the air as you read this—is called "Dave's World." It's loosely based on a book and some columns I wrote. I use the term "loosely" very loosely. There's no way they could just take my columns and turn them directly into a TV series; every episode would last four minutes, and end with all the major characters being killed by an exploding toilet. So they have professional writers supplying dramatic elements that are missing from my writing, such as plots, characters, and jokes that do not involve the term "toad mucus."

(Lest you think I have "sold out" as an artist, let me

stress that I have retained total creative control over the show, in the sense that, when they send me a check, I can legally spend it however I want.)

I worked hard on "Howdy," memorizing it in just days. Depending on the scene, I could deliver the line with various emotional subtexts, including happiness ("Howdy!"), sorrow ("Howdy!"), anger ("Howdy!"), and dental problems ("Hmpgh!").

Then, just before I flew to Los Angeles for the filming, the director called to tell me that they had changed my role. In my new role, I played a man in an appliance store who tries to buy the last air conditioner but gets into a bidding war for it with characters who are based, loosely, on

me and my wife, played by Harry Anderson and DeLane Matthews. (Harry Anderson plays me. Only taller.)

In my new role, I had to say 17 words, not ONE of which was "Howdy!" I was still memorizing my part when I got to the studio. It was swarming with people—camera people, light people, sound people, bagel people, cream-cheese people, people whose sole function—this is a coveted union job, passed down from father to son—is to go "SSHHH!" You, the actor, have to say your lines with all these people constantly staring at you, PLUS the director and the writers keep changing the script. The actors will do a scene, and the director will say, "OK, that was perfect, but this time, Bob, instead of saying 'What's for dinner?' you say, 'Wait a minute! Benzene is actually a hydrocarbon!' And say it with a Norwegian accent. Also, we think maybe your character should have no arms."

My lines didn't change much, but as we got ready to film my scene, I was increasingly nervous. I was supposed to walk up to the appliance salesman and say: "I need an air conditioner." I had gone over this many times, but as the director said "Action!" my brain—the brain is easily the least intelligent organ in the body—lost my lines, and began frantically rummaging around for them in my memory banks. You could actually see my skull bulging with effort as I walked onto the set, in front of four TV cameras, a vast technical crew, and a Live Studio Audience, with no real idea what I was going to say to the appliance salesman ("I need a howdy").

But somehow I remembered my lines. The director seemed satisfied with my performance, except for the last part, where Harry Anderson, outbidding me for the air conditioner, hands the salesman some takeout sushi and says, "We'll throw in some squid," and I become disgusted and say, "Yuppies." (If you recognize this dialogue, it's because it's very similar to the appliance-buying scene in *Hamlet*.)

"That was perfect, Dave," said the director. (This is what directors say when they think it sucked.) "But when you say 'yuppies,' make it smaller."

So we redid the scene, and as we approached my last line, I was totally focused on doing a smaller "yuppies." Then I noticed that (a) the other actors weren't saying anything, and (b) everybody in the studio was staring at me, waiting. I had clearly messed up, but I had no idea how. This was a time to think fast, to improvise, to come up with a clever line that would save the scene. So here's what I did: I fell down. (It's a nervous habit I have. Ask my wife.)

When I got up, I explained that I'd been waiting for Harry to say the squid line.

"They took that out," somebody said.

"They took out the *squid*?" I said. "The squid is *gone*?"

It turned out that everybody else knew this, including probably the Live Studio Audience. So we had to do that part again, with my brain feverishly repeating "No squid! Smaller yuppies!" (This would be a good slogan for a restaurant.)

That time we got through it, and my television career came to an end, and I went back to being, loosely, a newspaper columnist. I have not, however, ruled out the possibility of starring in a spinoff. I am thinking of a dramatic action series about a hero who, each week, tries to buy an air conditioner. I have a great line for ending this column, but I can't remember what it is.

A FAILURE TO
COMMUNICATE

Now that my son has turned 13, I'm thinking about writing a self-help book for parents of teenagers. It would be a sensitive, insightful book that would explain the complex, emotionally charged relationship between the parent and the adolescent child. The title would be: *I'm a Jerk; You're a Jerk.*

The underlying philosophy of this book would be that, contrary to what you hear from the "experts," it's a bad idea for parents and teenagers to attempt to communicate with each other, because there's always the risk that one of you will actually find out what the other one is thinking.

For example, my son thinks it's a fine idea to stay up until 3 A.M. on school nights reading what are called "suspense novels," defined as "novels wherein the most positive thing that can happen to a character is that the Evil Ones will kill him *before* they eat his brain." My son sees *no connection* between the fact that he stays up reading these books and the fact that he doesn't feel like going to school the next day.

"Rob," I tell him, as he is eating his breakfast in ex-

Raising your TEENAGER

ZZZ

treme slow motion with his eyes completely closed, so that he sometimes accidentally puts food into his ear, "I want you to go to sleep earlier."

"DAD," he says, using the tone of voice you might use when attempting to explain an abstract intellectual concept to an oyster, "you DON'T UNDERSTAND. I am NOT tired. I am ... *SPLOOSH*" (sound of my son passing out facedown in his Cracklin' Oat Bran).

Of course psychologists would tell us that falling asleep in cereal is normal for young teenagers, who need to become independent of their parents and make their own life decisions, which is fine, except that if my son made his own life decisions, his ideal daily schedule would be:

Midnight to 3 A.M.—Read suspense novels.

3 A.M. to 3 P.M.—Sleep.

3:15 P.M.—Order hearty breakfast from Domino's Pizza and put on loud hideous music recorded live in hell.

4 P.M. to midnight—Blow stuff up.

Unfortunately, this schedule would leave little room for, say, school, so we have to supply parental guidance ("If you don't open this door RIGHT NOW I will BREAK IT DOWN and *CHARGE IT TO YOUR ALLOWANCE*"), the result being that our relationship with our son currently involves a certain amount of conflict, in the same sense that the Pacific Ocean involves a certain amount of water.

At least he doesn't wear giant pants. I keep seeing young teenage males wearing *enormous* pants; pants that two or three teenagers could occupy simultaneously and still have room in there for a picnic basket; pants that a clown would refuse to wear on the grounds that they were too undignified. The young men wear these pants really low, so that the waist is about knee level and the pants butt drags on the ground. You could not be an effective criminal wearing pants like these, because you'd be unable to flee on foot with any velocity.

POLICE OFFICER: We tracked the alleged perpetrator from the crime scene by following the trail of his dragging pants butt.

PROSECUTOR: And what was he doing when you caught up with him?

POLICE OFFICER: He was hobbling in a suspicious manner.

What I want to know is, how do young people buy these pants? Do they try them on to make sure they DON'T fit? Do they take along a 570-pound friend, or a mature polar bear, and buy pants that fit HIM?

I asked my son about these pants, and he told me that mainly "bassers" wear them. "Bassers" are people who like a lot of bass in their music. They drive around in cars with four-trillion-watt sound systems playing recordings of what sound like aboveground nuclear tests, but with less of an emphasis on melody.

My son also told me that there are also people called "posers" who DRESS like "bassers," but are, in fact, secretly "preppies." He said that some "posers" also pose as "headbangers," who are people who like heavy-metal music, which is performed by skinny men with huge hair who stomp around the stage, striking their instruments and shrieking angrily, apparently because somebody has stolen all their shirts.

"Like," my son said, contemptuously, "some posers will act like they like Metallica, but they don't know *anything* about Metallica."

If you can imagine.

I realize I've mainly been giving my side of the parent-teenager relationship, and I promise to give my son's side, if he ever comes out of his room. Remember how the news media made a big deal about it when those people came out after spending two years inside Biosphere 2? Well, two years is *nothing*. Veteran parents assure me that teenagers routinely spend that long in the *bathroom*. In fact, veteran parents assure me that I haven't seen *anything* yet.

"Wait till he gets his driver's license," they say. "That's when Fred and I turned to heroin."

Yes, the next few years are going to be exciting and challenging. But I'm sure that, with love and trust and understanding, my family will get through them OK. At least *I* will, because I plan to be inside Biosphere 3.